W9-BVC-249

YOUR BATTLES BELONG TO THE LORD
STUDY GUIDE

JOYCE MEYER

Faith
Words

NEW YORK NASHVILLE

AURORA PUBLIC LIBRARY

Copyright © 2019 by Joyce Meyer

Cover copyright © 2019 by Hachette Book Group, Inc.

Hachette Book Group supports the right to free expression and the value of copyright. The purpose of copyright is to encourage writers and artists to produce the creative works that enrich our culture.

The scanning, uploading, and distribution of this book without permission is a theft of the author's intellectual property. If you would like permission to use material from the book (other than for review purposes), please contact permissions@hbgusa.com. Thank you for your support of the author's rights.

FaithWords
Hachette Book Group
1290 Avenue of the Americas, New York, NY 10104
faithwords.com
twitter.com/faithwords

First Edition: September 2019

FaithWords is a division of Hachette Book Group, Inc. The FaithWords name and logo are trademarks of Hachette Book Group, Inc.

The publisher is not responsible for websites (or their content) that are not owned by the publisher.

The Hachette Speakers Bureau provides a wide range of authors for speaking events. To find out more, go to www.hachettespeakersbureau.com or call (866) 376-6591.

Unless otherwise noted, Scriptures are taken from *The Amplified Bible* (AMP). *The Amplified Bible, Old Testament*, copyright © 1965, 1987 by The Zondervan Corporation. *The Amplified New Testament*, copyright © 1954, 1958, 1987 by The Lockman Foundation. Used by permission.

Scripture quotations marked (KJV) are taken from the *King James Version*. Public domain.

Scriptures marked (THE MESSAGE) are taken from *The Message: The Prophets* by Eugene Peterson. Copyright © 2000 by Eugene H. Peterson. NavPress Publishing Group, P.O. Box 35001, Colorado Springs, CO 80935. Used by permission.

Scriptures noted (NIV) are taken from the *Holy Bible: New International Version®*. Copyright © 1973, 1978, 1984 by International Bible Society. Used by permission of Zondervan Publishing House. All rights reserved.

Scripture quotations marked (NKJV) are taken from the *New King James Version*. Copyright © 1979, 1980, 1982 by Thomas Nelson, Inc., Publishers.

ISBN: 978-1-5460-2628-0

Printed in the United States of America

LSC-C

10 9 8 7 6 5 4 3 2 1

CONTENTS

Contents

INTRODUCTION

I believe most people are fighting something at one time or another, which is why the title of this book is probably very appealing to most of us. We are usually either in the middle of a battle, just finishing one, or heading into one. There are very few times we can say everything in our lives is working out perfectly.

The various trials, challenges, and problems we encounter in this world can be called our "battles" in life. Battles can be in our relationships, our finances, or our health. They may involve the death of a loved one or uncertainty about a decision we need to make. We live fast-paced lives and rarely have a day when everything goes as perfectly as we planned.

But Jesus never promised us a life without trouble or opposition. In fact, He promised just the opposite. He said that in the world we would have tribulation, distress, and suffering (see John 16:33). If we were to stop there, we would have to be discouraged, but Jesus also said that in Him we can have perfect peace...that we can be courageous, confident, undaunted, and filled with joy because He has overcome the world (see John 16:33).

In this book, we will unpack this Scripture and explore many others that can help us gain the victory in our battles. We'll learn some very practical things we can do to come against Satan, the one who comes to steal, kill, and destroy (see John 10:10), and how to employ strategies to let God fight for us. No matter how difficult our challenges are, if God is with us, we have all we need to win every battle. And we should always remember that all things are possible with God (see Matt. 19:26). His strength shows itself best through our weaknesses (see 2 Cor. 12:9), and the more we lean on Him, the more we will succeed at whatever we do.

This study guide has been designed as a companion to the book *Your Battles Belong to the Lord*. Read each chapter thoroughly in *Your Battles Belong to the Lord*, and then go through the corresponding chapter in this guide to learn how to make the strategies discussed in the book work for you.

As you take this journey, you'll be encouraged to meditate on the biblical principles that are presented and discover practical ways to apply them to your life. Each chapter includes the following sections:

Get Started

This helps you review what you've learned in the previous section as well as how you've applied it to your life. Then it presents a short exercise to get you thinking more about the current chapter.

Get Armed

This section opens up the chapter and gives you questions and exercises to help you think more deeply about the main concepts.

The Word

The Word section uses Scripture to help you explore the truth about the information in the chapter. Everything is based on God's Word, and learning the Scriptures will give you a solid foundation of truth and help you draw closer to God.

Take Action

This section contains exercises to help you apply what you're learning in the book. Review it often to keep you moving forward as you incorporate the principles and strategies in your daily life. Taking action and putting into practice what you're learning are key to gaining victory over your battles.

Remember

Lastly, I include takeaways from the book to help you remember what you should continue doing as you move forward. These sections include Scriptures that reinforce the main points of the chapter, and I encourage you to memorize them. They are powerful verses that will help you greatly when you are in the midst of battles.

As I write in *Your Battles Belong to the Lord*, when we let God fight our battles, we always win, but if we try to fight them ourselves, we always lose. However, it is important to understand that although our battles belong to the Lord, it does not mean we become passive, inactive, and lazy. While we need to wait to take action until God shows us what to do and when to do it, we must remain spiritually active in our faith with confident expectation that He is working and will show us our part in the warfare. As we learn to let God fight our battles, we can actually enjoy life while we are waiting for victory, and we can have peace in the depths of our being while storms rage in our circumstances.

In this book you will learn to know your enemy. You will learn to know his nature and tactics and how to recognize and defeat him. Martyn Lloyd-Jones wrote in his book *The Christian Warfare*, "What a wise teacher does is to expound the Epistles, especially concerning the teaching of the wiles of the devil. All of our problems arise ultimately from that source" (Carlisle, PA: Banner of Truth Trust, 1976, p. 99). I want you to know your enemy and to realize that you need not fear him. I also want you to be educated and equipped with all the information you need about his tactics, deceits, and schemes so you can recognize his attacks and defeat him.

It is obvious to anyone that two forces are at work in the world—good and evil. God is good, and the devil is evil. Since the devil cannot get to God to hurt Him, he fights against His children—those who have believed in Jesus as Savior and Lord and have been born again into His Kingdom. He hopes to hurt God through hurting us, but God has made His plan clear and it is simply this: "… The Son of God appeared for this purpose, to destroy the works of the devil" (1 John 3:8).

In Romans 12:21, the apostle Paul writes that we overcome evil with good. Our natural inclination would be to return evil for evil, but that is not how we win spiritual battles against the devil and his demon hosts. He hopes to anger us and provoke us to act out of that anger, but Jesus teaches us to love one another. Love is the most powerful force in the world; Satan has no way to win against true love. Paul writes in Acts 10:38 that Jesus went about doing good and healing all who were oppressed by the devil because God was with Him. He overcame evil with good, and we can too.

I believe you will learn through this study that not only does God want to fight our battles, He wants to teach us how to fight *in a way that assures victory*. Some of this may be surprising and seem that it simply cannot work, but God's ways always work if we remain steadfast in our determination to follow Him into battle and all the way through to victory!

Get ready to have your mind renewed and your thinking changed as you learn the truth of God's Word concerning the battles in your life. Your fight is not against people or even with circumstances, it is against the devil (see Eph. 6:12).

Your battles belong to the Lord, and the victory belongs to you! Remember that God is *with you* and *for you* in the midst of all your earthly struggles, and you will be more than a conqueror through Jesus Christ, who loves you (see Rom. 8:37).

CHAPTER 1

Know Your Enemy

Before you begin, please read Chapter 1 in Your Battles Belong to the Lord.

Get Started

Think about ways you are tempted repeatedly in life. Write them down to consider in a later activity.

Now read the opening Scripture, 1 Peter 5:8, from at least three different Bible translations and answer these questions:

1. Who does the Scripture say is your enemy?

_____

2. What animal is the devil compared to and why?

_____

_____

3. What does the verse say to you?

_____

_____

_____

_____

_____

Satan prowls around looking for someone to devour, but that person doesn't have to be you! If you get to know him and his tactics, and if you remain watchful and alert, you can avoid being deceived and trapped by him.

Get Armed

Read the story by Carl Armerding. What is the point of the illustration? How does it support the description of our enemy in 1 Peter 5:8?

_____

_____

_____

_____

Consider the statement: The devil is a liar, and he can only harm people who believe him and are deceived by him. What difference does this statement make in how you perceive the devil?

_____

_____

_____

_____

How did Jesus triumph over evil?

_____

_____

_____

Scripture helps us realize that we are fighting from a vantage point of already having victory, rather than trying to win a victory.

Write down any Scriptures from today's chapter or from your personal reading that remind you that Christ has already defeated the devil.

_____

_____

_____

The Word

Take some time and look into a figurative mirror. How do you see yourself? What phrases do you repeatedly say about yourself (to yourself or to others)?

_____

_____

_____

_____

The way we see ourselves is very important. We should see ourselves as people with authority, as conquerors and victorious believers. If we allow the devil to convince us that we are weak, incapable, unable, and losers, then we will believe and demonstrate those characteristics. We should agree with God and believe what He says about us.

One of Satan's main objectives is to prevent us from knowing who we are in Christ and knowing what our privileges are as children of God. He works tirelessly to try to make us feel bad about ourselves and believe we are not acceptable to God or anyone else. As I stated above, what we believe about ourselves is very important. It is more important than what anyone else thinks.

Look up the following Scriptures and then write them in your own words, describing who God created you to be.

Psalm 139:14:

_____

_____

Isaiah 49:16:

_____

_____

_____

Genesis 1:27:

_____

_____

_____

Ephesians 2:10:

_____

_____

_____

Read the account in Genesis 2:15–17. Write down what God told Adam.

_____

_____

_____

Now read Genesis 3:1–4. Write down what Eve said and then how the serpent responded.

_____

_____

_____

What are the differences in these accounts?

_____

_____

_____

Likewise, compare the words you've written down about yourself and the Scripture-based statements you have written. What are the differences?

_____

_____

_____

If we are unaware of Satan as a real threat and if we do not know his character, he can easily deceive us and we can end up believing many things that are not true. These beliefs will keep us from enjoying the life that Jesus died for us to have.

Take Action

Read the quote from Corrie ten Boom: "The first step on the way to victory is to recognize the enemy." How can recognizing the devil as your enemy help you on your road toward victory?

_____

_____

_____

What will you do to combat the enemy? How will you lessen the devil's voice in your head so you can believe God rather than the enemy?

_____

_____

_____

Why would believers give evil spirits the opportunity to attack their minds? They would do so only because they are ignorant of his wiles and methods of deception, or perhaps they are ignorant of his existence entirely. The word *wiley*, which is related to *wiles*, means cunning, crafty, and deceitful. Wiles are often described as "clever tricks," and they are Satan's way of gaining entrance into a person's life. Satan doesn't knock on the front door of our lives announcing his arrival, telling us who he is and informing us that he has come to destroy us. He lies in wait for an opportune time and then he lies, deceives, and cunningly and craftily makes his way in, often undetected. Then he delights in hearing us blame God or other people for the trouble the devil himself is instigating.

This week, pay particular attention to your thoughts, especially the thoughts you have about yourself. Write them down below and review them next week. Include a summary of what most of your thoughts are about.

_____

_____

_____

The Bible tells us to resist the devil (see James 4:7), but we often unknowingly assist him through receiving as our own any and every thought he puts into our minds. You and I can and should do our own thinking. We should choose our thoughts carefully because they ultimately become the blueprint for our lives.

Remember

Stop and ask yourself what lies you might be believing right now that are preventing you from entering into the fullness of the life Jesus wants you to have.

> Do not conform to the pattern of this world, but be transformed by the renewing of your mind. Then you will be able to test and approve what God's will is—his good, pleasing and perfect will. (Romans 12:2 NIV)

Do All the Crisis Demands

Before you begin, read Chapter 2 in Your Battles Belong to the Lord.

Get Started

Review your action steps from last week. How has knowing more about your enemy helped you, and what did you think about most? Are there any changes you need to make in your mind-set to help you live victoriously?

_____

_____

_____

_____

Focus on the opening Scripture in Chapter 2: Ephesians 6:13. Rewrite this verse in your own words; feel free to read several versions to help you with this.

_____

_____

_____

_____

Anytime we find ourselves in any kind of crisis, it's a battle in our lives. During these times we must not remain passive or neutral. We must act! We cannot do what we do not know to do, but God expects us to do what we can. I often say that if we do what we can do while leaning on God, He will do what we cannot do as we stand in faith waiting for Him to grant us full victory.

Get Armed

Think about a current battle you are fighting (or a recent battle). What are you doing or what did you do to get through it? How does the quote "God will fight our battles for us, but we have to show up for the fight" apply to your battle?

_____

_____

_____

_____

It is useless to know what to do if we do not actually do it. Some people procrastinate, thinking they will do what needs to be done, but their plan is to do it later. That type of thinking is deceptive, because for most of them, later is never a good time either. Procrastination is like a credit card—it is a lot of fun until you get the bill. Putting off easy things only makes them hard. Be a person of action; do what needs to be done and never put off until tomorrow what you should do today.

What can you do today while you're waiting for a resolution to your battle?

_____

_____

_____

The Word

Read about the man at the pool of Bethesda (see John 5:1–9). What stands out to you about this account?

_____

_____

_____

_____

I think the man was sicker in his soul than he was in his body. His attitude was filled with "I can't," and when that is the case for people, just like this man, they don't even try. I don't know how far the man could walk or even how often he managed the strength to walk at all, but surely in thirty-eight years he could have wiggled his way over to the edge of the pool to assure that he would be the first to fall into the water when the angel came.

Do you agree that the man was sicker in his soul than his body? Why or why not?

_____

_____

_____

Read the story of the ten virgins in Matthew 25. Explain how the five wise virgins symbolize those who do what they can do while waiting on God and the five foolish virgins did the opposite.

_____

_____

_____

Take Action

Read the list of examples I provide of things we can do while waiting for God to do what only He can do. Which ones apply to your situation and how?

_____

_____

_____

We should pray all the time, including times when we intend to take action. We should never take any kind of action without acknowledging God in it. For example, I might have prayed in the situation with my friend in need, "Father, _____ needs money to pay her rent this month because of an unexpected car repair. I am willing to pay it for her if that is what You would like me to do." Then if I sense peace about my intended action, I go ahead with it.

Spend time praying specifically about your battle. Below, keep track of ways you can stay active while waiting on God for the resolution you need.

_____

_____

_____

What message does the story about the barber and minister highlight about passive people who want God to fix all our problems? What does this story inspire you to do?

_____

_____

_____

Actually there are so many problems that they seem overwhelming, I admit; but perhaps of all of our problems, the biggest one is not doing what we could do. We cannot do it all, but we must refuse to do nothing.

Remember

God did not fill us with abilities, gifts, talents, strength, and creativity so we could sit around and do nothing. We either use what we have or we end up losing it.

For as the body apart from the spirit is dead, so also faith apart from works is dead. (James 2:26 ESV)

The Battle Belongs to the Lord

Before you begin, read Chapter 3 of Your Battles Belong to the Lord.

Get Started

What actions have you taken as you wait on God as a result of studying the previous chapter? What difference have you observed in your situation?

_____

_____

_____

Read the opening Scripture, 2 Chronicles 20:15. You may also read verses 1–14 to understand the context of what Jahaziel is saying to King Jehoshaphat.

How can your current battle or a recent battle be compared to a "vast army" (2 Chron. 20:15 NIV) coming against you?

_____

_____

_____

Rewrite the verse from 2 Chronicles 20:15 in your own words and apply it to your own battle.

_____

_____

_____

We should do what we can do and let God do what we cannot do.

Get Armed

What did Jehoshaphat do first after he heard about the vast army, or the great multitude?

_____

_____

_____

How have you sought the Lord for help with your battle?

_____

_____

_____

What else did Jehoshaphat do?

_____

_____

_____

How can you follow his example as you face, or as you're going through, your battle?

_____

_____

_____

Are there any other things that come to mind that you can do?

_____

_____

_____

How do you demonstrate total dependence on God in the midst of your battle?

_____

_____

_____

I hope you are seeing the wisdom Jehoshaphat used in approaching God. He had not yet made a petition for help with his problem, but he had sought God, fasted, given praise, and reminded God that He had given them the land. Only after doing all of that did he mention his problem, but once again he reminded God that He would not allow them to invade those nations when they came from Egypt. He led them to not destroy them, and now here they were rewarding them by coming to drive them out of the land God gave them as an inheritance.

The Word

How do you think Jehoshaphat felt when he heard from God through Jahaziel?

_____

_____

_____

How does John 15:5 apply to having total dependence on God?

_____

_____

_____

How much trouble do you have with trusting God and relying on Him?

_____

_____

_____

List at least two additional Scriptures that remind you to totally depend on God.

_____

_____

_____

Rewrite those Scriptures in your own words and use them to help you be mindful to depend more fully on God.

_____

_____

_____

Jesus says that apart from Him we can do nothing (see John 15:5), and the sooner we learn this truth, the more battles we will win. He is the Vine and we are the branches, and no branch can survive very long if it is separated from the Vine, which is its life source. I think it is wise to verbalize our dependence on God several times a day. "God, I need You. I am nothing without You, and I can do nothing without You." These are powerful confessions that please God and remind us of the position that belongs to Him in our lives, which is first place. God leads and we follow! Nothing works if that order is reversed.

Take Action

They were told to go out against their enemies, but they were also told they would not need to fight. In this verse God speaks something else of great importance, which we don't want to miss. He said, "Take your position." The people obviously knew what their position should be because the next verse says that "Jehoshaphat bowed with his face to the ground, and all Judah... fell down before the Lord, worshiping Him. The Levites, from the sons of the Kohathites and the sons of the Korahites, stood up to praise the Lord God of Israel, with a very loud voice" (2 Chron. 20:18–19).

What did "take your position" mean to the people?

_____

_____

_____

How often do you praise and worship God in the midst of your battles? What difference does it make?

_____

_____

_____

What do you think of J. Oswald Sanders's quote about evangelicals? Do you personally identify with what he's saying? If so, explain.

_____

_____

_____

Describe your definition of praise and worship.

_____

_____

_____

How does God fight the battle for Jehoshaphat and his army?

_____

_____

_____

How does their battlefield literally become their place of blessing?

_____

_____

_____

Have you seen any of your battlefields—the places you've struggled—become your place of blessing? If so, explain.

_____

_____

_____

How does the story of Jehoshaphat's army, as well as your own experiences, prepare you to handle current or future battles?

_____

_____

_____

Remember

If God gives you something to do, do it. And if He leads you to worship, be obedient to do that.

"Do not be afraid or discouraged because of this vast army. For the battle is not yours, but God's." (2 Chronicles 20:15 NIV)

Eliminate Fear

Before you begin, read Chapter 4 in Your Battles Belong to the Lord.

Get Started

What actions have you taken toward defeating your battles this week? What takeaways from studying this book and completing the exercises have you incorporated? What changes have you noticed?

_____

_____

_____

_____

_____

Read the opening quote from Dale Carnegie. How does it apply to what you've learned so far about dealing with your battles?

_____

_____

_____

_____

_____

The fact that many of the great men and women we read about in the Bible struggled with fear did not keep God from giving them something to do. We don't get to sit and watch the world go by just because we feel afraid. God has given us faith, and that is what we use to overcome fear. We can feel afraid and still step out and do great things by faith.

Get Armed

Fear will never stop trying to talk to us, but we don't have to take the counsel (advice) of our fears. Recognize fear for what it is—the devil trying to stop you from doing what you believe you should be doing.

Think of a time you had to do something in spite of your fear. What happened?

_____

_____

_____

What do you think General George Patton meant when he said: "I learned very early in my life never to take counsel of my fears"?

_____

_____

_____

How can recognizing fear for what it is—the devil trying to stop you from doing what you believe you should be doing—help you to overcome fear or at least not take counsel from fear?

_____

_____

_____

How many opportunities do you think you've missed because you listened to your fears instead of listening to God? List some below.

_____

_____

The Word

If you do not know Esther's story, read about her in the Book of Esther in the Old Testament. Read the passages of Scripture below and describe what is happening in them.

Esther 2:2–11:

_____

_____

Esther 2:17–22:

_____

_____

_____

Esther 3:1–13:

_____

_____

_____

Esther 4:1–17:

_____

_____

_____

Esther 7:1–10:

_____

_____

_____

How did Esther overcome her fear of approaching the king?

_____

_____

_____

Esther is a young woman we read about in the Bible who was asked to do something outside of her comfort zone, something she certainly wasn't expecting. When Esther received her instructions from God through her uncle, Mordecai, she was afraid she would be put to death if she took the action she was being asked to take. Her uncle did not take pity on her and release her from her duty, but he did tell her that she had a chance to help her people and that if she didn't do it, God would find someone else. Thankfully, she pressed through her fears and did as she was asked to do and ended up saving her nation.

Read Numbers 13:1–33.

What report did the majority of the men give?

_____

_____

What report did Caleb give?

_____

_____

_____

What was the difference between what Caleb believed and what the other men believed?

_____

_____

_____

It never matters what we don't have in our favor or even how outnumbered we are. The victory depends on God, not our circumstances! Sometimes God will even put us into a position where there is no way we can win without Him—just to make sure we don't give ourselves the credit for the victory. An excellent example of this is found in the story of Gideon.

Read Judges 6:11–18.

How did God see Gideon? (See v. 12.)

_____

_____

_____

How did Gideon see himself? (See v. 15.)

_____

_____

_____

Gideon's answers clearly show that he was blaming the Israelites' problems on God, and he was fearful rather than brave. God saw what he was capable of, but Gideon had lived in fear so long that he was totally unaware of his abilities and the fact that God was with him. He proceeded to list the reasons he was not qualified: "My family is the least significant in Manasseh, and I am the youngest (smallest) in my father's house" (Judg. 6:15).

Judges 7 tells how Gideon and his army defeated their enemies. Read this passage of Scripture and describe how their victory unfolded.

_____

_____

_____

Take Action

You can feel fear and still do anything you know you need to do, even if you "do it afraid."

How do Esther and Gideon's examples inspire you to trust God more and obey His leading even if you have to "do it afraid"? What do their stories reveal to you about the character of God?

_____

_____

_____

What do you feel called to do even though you may be afraid?

_____

_____

_____

How can you "give God what you don't have"?

_____

_____

How does 2 Corinthians 12:9 help you give your fears to God?

_____

_____

Even if we don't have much in the natural, with God on our side all we need is His presence and a little bit of courage. I urge you not to let fear steal your destiny. You will never know what you can do unless you step out and find out. You will fight many battles because your enemy—the devil—will not go down quietly and easily. He will fight you every step of the way, but the Greater One (God) lives in you, and He is greater than the one who comes against you (see 1 John 4:4).

How does the story of the buffalo and the lion help to remind you that God is always with you?

_____

_____

Which "relatives of fear" are you experiencing in your battles?

_____

_____

What are some practical ways you can resist the devil and overcome them?

_____

_____

_____

Remember

Always remember that God and all His mighty angels are with you, and they will fight for you if you will choose to stand your ground rather than running away in fear.

When I am afraid, I put my trust in you. (Psalm 56:3 NIV)

CHAPTER 5

Fully Assured

Before you begin, read Chapter 5 in Your Battles Belong to the Lord.

Get Started

What steps have you taken to overcome fear this week? What do you need to continue to do?

_____

_____

_____

Read the opening quote by Charles Spurgeon. Spend some time meditating on the phrase *full assurance*. Then write your thoughts about what it means to have the "full assurance that [God] will never let [you] go."

_____

_____

_____

The Bible teaches us that we are to approach God in full assurance of faith (see Heb. 10:22), but Satan works tirelessly to steal our assurance and cause us to doubt and feel uncertain not only about our salvation, but about many other things too.

We are told to beware of the "wiles" of the devil, and this lack of assurance is one of them. It is one way he cunningly and craftily attacks us and distracts us from our purpose and calling, as well as preventing us from fully enjoying our relationship with God.

Get Armed

Think about how Satan works to steal your assurance of God's faithfulness and create doubt in your mind. Write some of the ways you've allowed Satan to make you doubt God's love for you and His desire to make you succeed in fulfilling His purpose and plan for your life.

_____

_____

_____

Why do you think Satan attacked you in these areas?

_____

_____

_____

How does having complete, full assurance in God help you live in His rest?

_____

_____

_____

In the midst of your battles, what is the state of your soul? Are you living in peace and experiencing the joyful expectation of good things to come today?

_____

_____

_____

Spend some time meditating on Matthew 19:26 and 1 Corinthians 10:13, reading them in several translations. How do these truths encourage you today?

_____

_____

_____

Complete and full assurance allows us to enter the rest of God, which means we can be at peace and fully enjoy our lives while we wait on God to do what we are trusting Him to do. However, the devil wants us to be anxious, worried, and fearful. Just think for a few moments about how wonderful your life could be if you had full assurance that God hears and answers your prayers, that you are saved and no one can snatch you from God's hand, that you are loved unconditionally, and that God will never allow more to come on you than what you can endure (see 1 Cor. 10:13). We need full assurance, not some assurance mixed with some doubt! Putting thoughts of doubt into our minds is one way Satan deceives us.

The Word

Read Romans 4. Pay particular attention to the passages that talk about Abraham's faith. Describe what God promised Abraham and then describe his faith.

_____

_____

_____

What made Abraham righteous?

_____

_____

_____

How can Abraham's faith serve as a model for you?

_____

_____

_____

Read 1 Timothy 6:12 and James 4:7 from several translations. Write what these verses mean to you and think of practical ways you will resist the devil when doubt creeps into your mind.

_____

_____

_____

When doubt comes, do you habitually resist the devil, reminding him that he is a liar? Do you reaffirm your faith in God by holding fast to a positive confession taken from one of the thousands of God's promises? Or do you passively receive the thoughts of doubt and merely "wish" you were stronger in faith? Wishing is useless because it has nothing to base its desires on, whereas faith can rest on the promises of God.

Take Action

Peter, Paul, and the other disciples continued to grow spiritually while God was using them. We mature spiritually little by little. While that process is taking place, we do improve in many ways, but we continue to have weaknesses to deal with. Let me simply say that you can still enjoy yourself while you are growing spiritually. God knew every mistake you would ever make before you made it, and He loves you anyway. Don't let Satan convince you that you have lost your salvation when you display immature behavior. Be quick to repent and ask the Holy Spirit to help you grow spiritually.

Do you believe it is possible to enjoy yourself while you are growing spiritually and dealing with weaknesses? Explain why or why not.

_____

_____

_____

Study Philippians 1:6 and 3:13 in several translations. What do these verses reveal about the process we all must go through to become everything God has created us to be?

_____

_____

_____

Do you need to let go of the guilt of past sins? If so, write a prayer below and ask God for help to accept complete forgiveness and restoration.

_____

_____

_____

We must learn to walk in continual forgiveness of our sins. Daily repentance should be part of our prayers. King David asked God to forgive him for sins he was unaware of (see Ps. 19:12), and I often do that myself. I learned long ago that it was unfruitful for me to live with a "sin consciousness," always being conscious of every tiny mistake I made. When I become aware that I have sinned, I quickly repent. Then, believing I have been forgiven according to God's promise in His Word, I forget it and go on to better things.

Describe the difference between a "righteousness conscience" and a "sin conscience."

_____

_____

_____

Do you have a righteousness conscience in your relationship with Christ? Explain how you will develop this mind-set and attitude if you struggle with this.

_____

_____

_____

Are you angry with anyone? If you are, pray and choose to forgive that person now. Write any reflections you have below after praying.

_____

_____

_____

Ask yourself daily if you are angry with anyone, and if the Holy Spirit makes you aware that you are, then decide right then and there to forgive completely. Ask for God's help in doing so, and trust Him to bring justice in your life. Pray for your enemies, that God would bless them, because this is one of the single most powerful things you can do. If Jesus can forgive us for our many sins, then we should be able to forgive anyone else, no matter what they have done to hurt us.

Read the parable of the Prodigal Son in Luke 15:11–32. What does the story reveal to you about forgiveness?

_____

_____

_____

Write one way you will rejoice in God's plan of salvation and forgiveness this week.

_____

_____

_____

Remember

We do have trials and tribulations, but as Paul said, we should not allow the difficulty of these momentary afflictions to distract us from the joy that is ours in Christ.

> Rejoice in the Lord always [delight, take pleasure in Him]; again I will say, rejoice! (Philippians 4:4)

CHAPTER 6

Assurance Concerning Prayer

Before you begin, read Chapter 6 from Your Battles Belong to the Lord.

Get Started

Since studying the previous chapter, do you find that you have more confidence and assurance of God's love and faithfulness to you? Explain why or why not and note ways you'll continue to grow in this area of your faith in Him.

_____

_____

_____

Begin by reading the opening quote: "To be a Christian without prayer is no more possible than to be alive without breathing." Share your thoughts on why prayer is vitally essential to the Christian life.

_____

_____

_____

Evaluate your prayer life. Write about how often you pray and how connected to God you feel when you pray. What would you like to improve in your prayer life?

_____

_____

_____

Christians are meant to know joy and peace, and that isn't possible unless we know how to pray and have full assurance of the power of prayer. God actually needs our prayers because there is a great deal He desires to do and cannot do unless someone asks Him to do it. It seems impossible that God would need us for anything, but since He works through us, He does need us. Obviously God can do anything He chooses to without anyone's help, but He has committed Himself to partnership with His children, and that is amazing.

Get Armed

Reflect on the story about prayers that stick. Do you pray with assurance that God hears and answers your prayers? Why or why not?

_____

_____

_____

_____

On a scale of 1 to 5, how much joy and peace do you have on a daily basis? (1 is none and 5 is the most you can have.)

1   2   3   4   5

Why did you choose that number?

_____

_____

_____

_____

Read Ephesians 3:20. What does this verse reveal to you about how God wants to use you?

_____

_____

_____

Do you believe God is able to do far more than we can imagine or ask? Explain your answer.

_____

_____

_____

_____

What distractions do you encounter when you try to pray?

_____

_____

_____

What ways can you avoid those distractions or ignore them?

_____

_____

_____

My prayers are usually simple, but they are sincere. I think the devil wants us to believe that prayer should always be hard work and that we need to feel deep emotion concerning what we pray about. That may be the case at times, but it is the sincerity of our prayers and the faith offered with them that makes them effective, not what we feel, or whether we cry or not, or how loud or long we pray. Be cautious not to let the devil deceive you concerning the validity of your prayers. When you pray in faith, God hears and He answers in His way and in His timing.

The Word

Read the following Scriptures mentioned in this chapter and describe how each person prayed.

Luke 22:44:

_____

_____

_____

Colossians 4:12:

_____

_____

_____

God's will is for us to be able to pray with confidence and assurance. Our prayers are not meant to be uncertain. We are not meant to be vague and doubtingly groping after God, hoping we may get lucky and get an answer to our request. No! This is not true prayer. This kind of prayer doesn't receive answers from God. We are not slinging mud balls with prayer requests written on pieces of paper at God, hoping they will stick.

According to James 1:5–8, what should our mind-set and attitude be when we pray to God for wisdom and help?

_____

_____

_____

_____

What does James say about a double-minded and unstable person? Why?

_____

_____

_____

Read 1 John 5:14–15 from several translations. How do these verses encourage you to have confidence and assurance when praying?

_____

_____

_____

Look for Scriptures this week to use in your prayers. You will write a few prayers based on them in the next section.

Read the "Wow" Scriptures I present in the book. Which one of them speaks to you the most? Why?

_____

_____

_____

_____

Read about the hindrances to answered prayer. Which ones do you think are hindering your prayers? Spend time talking to God now about those hindrances. Feel free to write some thoughts below.

_____

_____

_____

I think it is safe to say that overcoming selfishness is a lifetime challenge. I never have to try to be selfish, but I often have to make an intentional decision not to be selfish. Even in prayer, I think our natural inclination is to pray for what we want and need first and foremost. But if we remember the prayer of Jehoshaphat, we will recall that his request was at the bottom of his list, while praise and gratitude were at the top.

Take Action

What books on prayer have you read or want to read to keep your faith fresh and strong concerning prayer? Ask a friend or someone you trust and respect spiritually to recommend some if you do not know of any.

_____

_____

_____

Order the book or make time to go to the library for it this week.
Who do you want to pray for this week? Keep a list of other people you want to pray for moving forward as God puts them on your heart.

_____

_____

_____

I remember reading a statement from Watchman Nee, saying that most of the ground Satan gains in the lives of believers is due to the fact that they are not willing to forgive those who have hurt them or treated them unfairly.

Prayer is far too important for us to allow these obstacles or anything else to hinder its effectiveness. Oh God, let us be assured of the power of prayer and help us pray often.

Write a prayer based on two Scriptures. You can choose ones we've studied in this chapter or others that reveal promises from God. Write your prayers below.

_____

_____

_____

If you're struggling with forgiving someone who has hurt you, ask God to help you forgive them so you can have full assurance that He hears and will answer your prayers.

Remember

If we focus on the great faith we do have rather than the little bit of doubt we may have, I believe we will also see answers to our prayers.

> "Whenever you stand praying, if you have anything against anyone, forgive him [drop the issue, let it go], so that your Father who is in heaven will also forgive you your transgressions and wrongdoings [against Him and others]." Mark 11:25

Ways the Devil Tries to Deceive People

Before you begin, read Chapter 7 in Your Battles Belong to the Lord.

Get Started

Since completing the previous chapter, think about how your prayer life has changed. Share any insights below.

_____

_____

_____

_____

Read the opening Scripture from Revelation 12:9. How is Satan described here, and why is his impact on people so dangerous?
How does Satan devour people through deception?

_____

_____

_____

Satan devours people through deception. When we are deceived, we believe lies we have been told, but since we do not know they are lies, we accept them as truth and act according to them. It is imperative that children of God know the difference between the lies of Satan and the truth of God's Word; otherwise they can be kept in bondage all of their lives. They will also miss out on the privileges and wonderful lives God has planned for them.

Get Armed

Read the examples given of how deception operates. Are you believing any of these things? If so, write them down and then write a prayer asking God to help you believe His truth that counteracts those lies.

_____

_____

_____

_____

Why is prayer one of our first defenses against deception?

_____

_____

_____

Explain what this quote means: If you don't stand for something, you will fall for anything.

_____

_____

_____

Why is this a dangerous position to be in?

_____

_____

_____

Describe the difference between relative and absolute truth.

_____

_____

_____

What is your source of absolute truth?

_____

_____

_____

Society today continually sends us the message that there is no absolute truth, but that truth is ever changing and based on our perceptions. In other words, the truth can be one thing to one person and something else to another. Of course, that is nonsense because if truth exists at all, it is a constant standard that is the same all the time for all people.

Personally I believe God's Word is absolute truth. My understanding of His Word may grow and change as I study and am taught, but His Word is always the same. It is the standard on which I base all of my decisions and by which I measure my thoughts. It is the only way I know to recognize the lies of the devil and to prevent myself from being deceived.

The Word

Read Matthew 24:4 and Matthew 24:24 from several translations. Write what the verses say to you.

_____

_____

_____

Read 1 John 4:1. How do you "test the spirits" to see if they are from God?

_____

_____

_____

Test what you hear, read and believe. Ask if it agrees with God's Word and if it truly works in your life and produces good fruit. Find the truth and hold it firmly in your heart and never let it go.

Read John 14:6. Do you believe that Jesus is the Way, the Truth, and the Life? If not, write your thoughts below and pray about them. You may also want to share your concerns with a person you trust and respect spiritually who trusts that God's Word is absolute truth.

_____

_____

_____

Study Hebrews 13:8 in several translations. How does this describe God's nature and encourage us to know He is the only source of absolute truth?

_____

_____

_____

Take Action

Read the list of practical ways to avoid deception. Which ones do you need to work on to avoid deception? Write a plan for how you will do this in the coming week.

_____

_____

_____

More than anything, people tell us how they feel, but feelings don't always tell us the truth. They are fickle! We may feel like doing one thing at 8:00 A.M. and somehow by 2:00 P.M. we no longer feel like doing it, even though we said we would do it earlier. Victorious Christians must learn how to manage our emotions and how to judge what we feel by God's Word to determine whether our feelings are conveying truth or deception.

Read 2 Timothy 2:4 from several translations. How does this verse help you resist the temptation to live a life of compromise?

_____

_____

_____

What does Psalm 37:4 tell us to do to ensure our desires line up with what God has planned for us and what is best for us?

_____

_____

_____

How can ungodly desires lead you to frustration and unfulfillment?

_____

_____

_____

What things have you desired that have never delivered the happiness or lasting satisfaction you craved? Why was this the case?

_____

_____

_____

Like most people, I tried all the wrong ways to find happiness until I finally exhausted all possibilities and then, thankfully, I learned that my own desires were deceiving me. Satan was continually whispering to me, "This is it, this will make you happy once you get it." He is a liar. What we truly need to find true happiness is God and His will for our lives.

Remember

God wants us to have many enjoyable things, but He must be first place in our lives. God can give us joy without things, but things without God will never give us joy.

> Put on the full armor of God [for His precepts are like the splendid armor of a heavily-armed soldier], so that you may be able to [successfully] stand up against all the schemes and the strategies and the deceits of the devil. (Ephesians 6:11)

CHAPTER 8

Hold Your Peace

Before you begin, read Chapter 8 in Your Battles Belong to the Lord.

Get Started

What ways have you implemented to avoid giving in to Satan's deception? What else will you do moving forward?

_____

_____

_____

_____

Think about the opening Scripture from Exodus 14:14. Write down your thoughts about what it means. How can it help you live victoriously?

_____

_____

_____

_____

What does it mean to "hold your peace"?

_____

_____

_____

_____

When we cut away everything that distracts us, I think what most of us want more than anything else is peace, and according to Jesus, we have it.

Get Armed

What challenges you most when it comes to holding your peace (keeping silent or remaining calm)?

_____

_____

_____

_____

God will fight our battles for us, but we see in Exodus 14:14 that we have a responsibility, which is to hold on to our peace. The Amplified Classic version of this says we are to "keep silent and remain calm." Is this challenging? Yes! Is it possible? Yes! God never tells us to do something that is not possible for us to do. It is important to believe that, otherwise the devil will fill our minds with endless excuses and reasons we cannot do what God tells us to do.

Do you agree that what we want more than anything else is peace? Explain why or why not.

_____

_____

_____

Think of a time you remained peaceful in the midst of a battle. How did things work out for you in the end?

_____

_____

_____

What did you learn about the power of God's peace through the situation you just wrote about?

_____

_____

_____

The Word

Read the following Scriptures from several versions of the Bible and write what they reveal to you about God's peace and how it greatly improves our lives.

John 14:27:

_____

_____

_____

Romans 16:20:

_____

_____

_____

Isaiah 9:6:

_____

_____

_____

Matthew 5:9:

_____

_____

_____

When trouble comes, we can think about all the terrible things that could happen, or we can choose to think that God is faithful and that He will fight our battles for us while we continue trusting Him and being a blessing to others. When we fail, we can imagine that God is angry with us, or we can believe what God's Word teaches us about God's forgiveness and mercy. Likewise, when people upset or disappoint us, we can meditate on their offense, but the longer we do so, the angrier we will become. Or we can choose to think about the value of the person and the good things we enjoy about them. We can also choose to believe the best rather than the worst. For example, some people are not even aware they hurt us. They may be going through something painful themselves, and what they said or did was birthed out of their own pain. Maybe they need encouragement instead of isolation.

Take Action

List some strategies you can use to keep calm.

_____

_____

_____

You may remember that Exodus 14:14 says to remain silent, and God will fight for you. This is because we sometimes talk too much to the wrong people, or out of our frustration and fear, we say things that do not agree with God's Word. The best thing to do during a battle is to meditate on Scriptures that will help you calm down. Anytime I start to worry, I meditate on Philippians 4:6, which tells me to be anxious for nothing, but in all things, by prayer, to let my requests be made known to God with thanksgiving, and then the peace that passes understanding will keep my heart and mind in Christ.

Read the quote by Ronald Reagan: *Peace is not the absence of conflict, it is the ability to handle conflict by peaceful means.* What does it mean to handle conflict by peaceful means?

_____

_____

_____

How will learning to handle conflict peacefully impact your daily living?

_____

_____

_____

Do you tend to worry more or pray and meditate on God's Word more? Write a plan to pray and keep your focus on the truth of Scripture more.

_____

_____

Read 1 John 3:8, Matthew 28:18, and Ephesians 1:18–23. What was Jesus' purpose in coming to Earth, and what is our hope and inheritance as believers and disciples of Christ?

_____

_____

_____

How can you use the power and authority of Christ to remain peaceful and calm during storms?

_____

_____

_____

How does worry empty today of its strength?

_____

_____

_____

How do you pursue peace with God, yourself, and others?

_____

_____

_____

Peace with God is found in repentance and receiving forgiveness for sins. We find it through developing an intimate relationship with God and realizing that He cares deeply about every area of our lives and wants to be involved in everything we do. We discover it as we come to know how much God loves us and how precious we are to Him. Receiving God's forgiveness and love allows us to learn how to forgive and love ourselves and how to be at peace with ourselves. Not one of us deserves God's help, but we can receive it by faith as a gift from Him because He is good!

Write a commitment statement about how you will pursue and hold on to your peace, incorporating strategies from this chapter.

_____

_____

_____

Remember

As frustrating as people can be, we need them and have to find a way to dwell together in unity or we will give the devil a foothold in our lives.

> Now we who are strong [in our convictions and faith] ought to [patiently] put up with the weaknesses of those who are not strong, and not just please ourselves. (Romans 15:1)

CHAPTER 9

What Is the Real Problem?

Before you begin, read Chapter 9 in Your Battles Belong to the Lord.

Get Started

On a scale of 1 to 5 (with 5 being the best), how successful have you been at holding your peace in the midst of storms? Moving forward, what strategies will you practice to help you maintain peace of mind and peace in your relationships when hard times come?

_____

_____

_____

Read Ephesians 6:12. Who is our real enemy in every battle we face?

_____

_____

_____

What happens when we forget that the devil is the source of misery, hatred, and the battles we fight?

_____

_____

_____

If we never learn what our real problem is, we will spend our lives fighting with things and people, yet never solving anything. The devil loves it when we don't know or remember that he is the source of all misery, hatred, strife, turmoil, and of the battles we fight. If we don't know that the devil exists and that he is our enemy, we live in great deception. He is against everything godly and good, and he is especially against God and His children (you and me).

Get Armed

Do you believe Satan works through people? Explain why or why not.

_____

_____

_____

_____

    Satan works through various means. He works through people, even good and well-meaning people, and he creates and works through circumstances of all kinds. Satan is behind all sin, all war, all strife, all disobedience, and everything that is not in agreement with God and His Word.

The Word

Paul begins Ephesians 6:12 by saying that we war not with flesh and blood, but with principalities and power and wickedness in high places. If our warfare (problem) is not with flesh and blood, then who is it with? Obviously, our problems are instigated by the devil and his demons. They definitely can and do work through people and circumstances to frustrate us, cause worry and anxiety, and lead to the loss of peace and joy.

Read the Scriptures that show Satan influencing people in ungodly ways. What was the outcome of each of these situations?

Matthew 16:21–23:

_____

_____

_____

Acts 5:1–11:

_____

_____

_____

Luke 22:1–6:

_____

_____

_____

Read what happened to the devil (Lucifer) in Isaiah 14:12–21 in several translations. Write what happened, and why, in your own words.

_____

_____

_____

List some of the spiritual weapons we've been given to defeat Satan.

_____

_____

_____

Take Action

What are some Scriptures you can use to resist the devil?

_____

_____

_____

What does "power of attorney" mean? How has Jesus given us power of attorney?

_____

_____

_____

_____

What does Jesus' name mean to you?

_____

_____

_____

Think of a saying or declaration like "This will end well" to use when you need a reminder that God is working on your behalf. Write it below.

_____

_____

_____

What spiritual weapons will you specifically use this week when you face a battle?

_____

_____

_____

Weapons are what we go after the enemy with; they are offensive tools. We speak the name of Jesus, believing in the power that is in that name. We remind the devil of the blood of Christ that defeated him when Jesus died and rose from the dead. We speak the Word of God. We overcome evil with good. We are promptly obedient to God. We worship God and sing His praises. And we do all of this while we are hurting or struggling in a battle. Doing what is right when everything is going right for us is good, but doing right when all is going wrong for us is a powerful weapon that ultimately defeats the devil.

Remember

The name of Jesus is above every other name and carries tremendous power.

> Therefore God exalted him to the highest place and gave him the name that is above every name, that at the name of Jesus every knee should bow, in heaven and on earth and under the earth. (Philippians 2:9–10 NIV)

CHAPTER 10
Dressed for Battle

Before you begin, read Chapter 10 in Your Battles Belong to the Lord.

Get Started

What weapons did you use this week to defeat Satan? Review the descriptions of our spiritual weapons in Chapter 9 and list the ones you need to be more mindful of moving forward.

_____

_____

_____

Read Ephesians 6:10–18. List the parts of the armor of God.

_____

_____

_____

The term *put on* is used several times in God's Word, and it is an action phrase. It requires us to do something. When I go to my closet each morning, my clothes don't jump off the rack and onto my body. I carefully select them and then I put them on. I check in the mirror to see if I think they look right on me, and if they don't, I change clothes.

Get Armed

How do you know when a Christian is wearing the armor of God? Explain.

_____

_____

_____

What behaviors do you sometimes wear that are not a good representation of Christ? Why?

_____

_____

_____

Why do we need faith to "put on" our armor?

_____

_____

_____

Since the armor is invisible, one might ask, "How do I put on something I cannot see?" The armor is spiritual and functions to protect us in the spiritual war. The way to put it on is by faith. Believe you have these powerful pieces of armor and walk in obedience to each of the principles they represent.

Think more about the armor of God and how we put it on. Answer the following questions:

What is the belt of truth and how do you use it in battle?

_____

_____

_____

How does the breastplate of righteousness help us fight battles?

_____

_____

_____

Knowing who we are in Christ is imperative if we are to defeat the devil. If he can keep us feeling guilty and condemned, he rules over us, but knowing who we are in Christ makes us strong and gives us an advantage over the enemy. He may tell us countless lies about ourselves, all negative things he wants us to believe, but knowing the truth of our identity in Christ keeps us walking in truth and defeating the lies of the devil. To know that we are the righteousness of God in Christ means that even though we don't do everything right, we are still viewed as being right through our faith. We are not condemned by our faults, but we are thankful when God reveals them because that means we can work with the Holy Spirit, who seeks to set us free and strengthen us.

What purpose do shoes serve?

_____

How do shoes of peace protect us?

_____

_____

_____

How do we "lift up" the shield of faith, and how does it help us?

_____

_____

_____

_____

Angels hearken to God's Word (see Ps. 103:20); they don't listen to nor are they moved to help us when we complain or speak words of fear, doubt, and unbelief. We are told to hold fast our confession of faith (see Heb. 10:23) during times of trouble and distress.

How can the helmet of salvation help us in battles?

_____

_____

_____

_____

The Word

God's Word is referred to as the sword of the Spirit. As we speak the Word, it is like a sword going forth from our mouths, protecting us and attacking our enemy the devil. Satan hates to be reminded of God's promises.

How did Jesus use the Word of God, or the sword of the Spirit, in each instance?

Matthew 4:1–4:

_____

_____

_____

Matthew 4:5–7:

_____

_____

_____

Matthew 4:8–10:

_____

_____

_____

How did Satan respond after his three defeats? (See Matt. 4:11.)

_____

_____

_____

Take Action

What Scriptures can serve as your sword in battle?

_____

_____

_____

How can you lift up your shield of faith in a battle you're in now?

_____

_____

_____

How can your attitude or mind-set keep you in peace during your battle?

_____

_____

_____

Ask yourself the following questions each morning. Write down any thoughts you have about how you can be more proactive in doing these things throughout your day.

Am I believing and walking in the truth?

_____

_____

_____

Do I see myself as the righteousness of God in Christ?

_____

_____

_____

Am I walking in peace?

_____

_____

_____

Am I living by faith by praying, saying, and doing God's Word in all areas of my life?

_____

_____

_____

Am I thinking like a child of God?

_____

_____

_____

_____

Am I regularly studying God's Word?

_____

_____

_____

Have I developed the habit of praying my way through the day?

_____

_____

_____

Remember

Reading and studying the book (the Bible) is one of the best investments of time we can ever make.

> Therefore, put on every piece of God's armor so you will be able to resist the enemy in the time of evil. Then after the battle you will still be standing firm. Stand your ground, putting on the belt of truth and the body armor of God's righteousness. For shoes, put on the peace that comes from the Good News so that you will be fully prepared. In addition to all of these, hold up the shield of faith to stop the fiery arrows of the devil. Put on salvation as your helmet, and take the sword of the Spirit, which is the word of God. Pray in the Spirit at all times and on every occasion. Stay alert and be persistent in your prayers for all believers everywhere. (Ephesians 6:13–18 NLT)

CHAPTER 11

Strength for the Battle

Before you begin, read Chapter 11 in Your Battles Belong to the Lord.

Get Started

Read Ephesians 6:10. How has putting on the armor helped you be strong in the Lord? How does the armor of God help you defeat the devil?

_____

_____

_____

What areas of spiritual warfare—the ways the armor of God is designed to help you—do you need to work on with God's help?

_____

_____

_____

Read the Amplified Bible version of Ephesians 6:10 below. What does "be strong in the Lord" mean to you, according to this translation? Explain it in your own words.

_____

_____

_____

I love the Amplified Bible version of Ephesians 6:10, which reads: "In conclusion, be strong in the Lord [draw your strength from Him and be empowered through your union with Him] and in the power of His [boundless] might."

Our strength is in Christ. He is in us and we are in Him. We draw our strength from Him as we live in close, intimate relationship with Him.

Get Armed

Think about the word *union*. What words come to mind when you think of this word? Write them below.

_____

_____

_____

_____

Now use these words to describe your relationship with Christ.

_____

_____

_____

In other words, God's strength doesn't merely come to those who go to church and believe that God exists and that Jesus was His Son, Who died for our sins. God's strength comes to those who are doing life with Him, in Him, and through Him. They know they can do nothing without Him and they don't waste their time trying to. Paul said, "In Him we live and move and exist [that is, in Him we actually have our being]" (Acts 17:28). That doesn't sound like a casual relationship, but a very committed and serious one.

Do you have a casual relationship with God or a committed relationship? Use the space below to draw where you think your relationship with God is. Then write about how you want to pursue a more committed, intimate connection with Him.

Casual _____ **Committed**

_____

_____

_____

The Word

Read John 15:5–8 from several versions of the Bible. Write what the verses mean to you and draw a picture below.

_____

_____

_____

Read the following passages that talk about God's strength or power working in our lives. What is each passage saying to you?

Philippians 4:13:

_____

_____

_____

2 Corinthians 12:7–10:

_____

_____

_____

_____

2 Corinthians 10:3–5:

_____

_____

_____

_____

Read 1 John 4:4 from several versions.

Write down the one that you want to memorize and commit it to memory.

_____

_____

    Satan's power is no match for the power of the Holy Spirit. God never asks us to do anything without giving us the power to do it. He has commanded us to resist and stand firmly against the devil and his demonic forces, and we have what it takes to do it as long as we remember that God is our strength.

Read Romans 8:37–39. What does it mean to you to be more than a conqueror?

_____

_____

Read the following verses from several versions. Write down a version of each that you will use to memorize them.
Isaiah 40:29:

_____

_____

_____

Isaiah 40:31:

_____

_____

_____

Isaiah 41:10:

_____

_____

_____

2 Thessalonians 3:3:

_____

_____

_____

Take Action

Christ is the Head, and we believers are considered His body because we are the ones walking the earth, being the hands and feet of Jesus. We are doing in His name the work He began while He was here on Earth. If all things are under His feet, then they are under our feet because we are His body. The knowledge of these spiritual truths should give us a quiet, yet powerful confidence that enables us to resist all opposition and do mighty things in Jesus' name and for His glory.

Evaluate your heart and what you believe; be honest with yourself and write how you really feel. On the last few lines, write a prayer asking God to help you in any area where you have doubt.

Are you confident, courageous, not easily defeated, determined, and bold?

_____

_____

_____

_____

Are you strength-minded? Do you believe you can do all things through Christ, who is your strength?

_____

_____

_____

_____

Do you see yourself as someone with authority, someone who is the head and not the tail? Explain why or why not.

_____

_____

_____

_____

As believers in Christ, with His power and authority, we can live ordinary life in an extraordinary way. The authority we have gives us the ability to have peace in the midst of the storm, joy in difficult circumstances, and certainty when everything around us is shaking.

My Prayer

_____

_____

_____

Based on your answers above and your prayer, what is God showing you to do moving forward?

_____

_____

_____

Remember

Hold your head up high and go through life expecting good things to happen to you and through you.

Then Jesus came to them and said, "All authority in heaven and on earth has been given to me." (Matthew 28:18 NIV)

The Importance of Watchfulness

Before you begin, read Chapter 12 in Your Battles Belong to the Lord.

Get Started

What steps have you taken to walk in your God-given authority since reading the last chapter? What more would you like to do?

_____

_____

_____

_____

Begin by reading 1 Peter 5:8 from several translations. Rewrite the verse in your own words.

_____

_____

_____

_____

What do the words *watchful* and *sober-minded* mean to you?

_____

_____

_____

_____

Get Armed

In what areas do you think you are watchful?

_____

_____

_____

In what areas do you need to become or be more watchful?

_____

_____

_____

As we walk through this world, it pays to be watchful in all areas, and it especially pays to watch out for the devil so he doesn't slither into our lives and deceive us. There is almost no limit to the ways—both big and little—that the devil conspires to ruin God's work and attack His people. He desires and works hard to bring Christians into bondage and unhappiness.

Do you agree that accepting Jesus as your Savior doesn't mean you'll have a trouble-free life? Explain.

_____

_____

_____

What does this quote mean to you: "Your worst day with Jesus will be better than your best day ever was without Him"? Do you agree? Explain why or why not.

_____

_____

_____

What books have you read about spiritual warfare? Which ones were most helpful and why?

_____

_____

_____

We need writing and teaching on the wiles of the devil and especially about the ways he attempts to afflict believers. If we are forewarned, we can be forearmed. If we understand how the enemy comes against us, and if we know how to resist him, we can be ready to combat his attacks instead of taken by surprise and defeated. This is one reason I have written this book.

The Word

Read Exodus 13:17. Why did God lead the Israelites through the wilderness?

_____

_____

_____

Read Hosea 4:6. What causes people to be destroyed? Why?

_____

_____

_____

How can you avoid this disastrous outcome?

_____

_____

_____

Read Deuteronomy 28:7 from several translations. What does this verse say to you?

_____

_____

_____

Memorize one of the translations of Deuteronomy 28:7 so you can recall it when the enemy attacks.

God knows that if we are fearful and turn back every time life becomes difficult, we will never possess what Jesus died to give us, so He works with us and teaches us to know our enemy and to be assured that he may come against us one way, but will flee from us seven ways (see Deut. 28:7). We need confidence in God, and that comes only as we experience His deliverance. Each time we have a problem and we trust God and see victory, we become a little bit stronger and Satan's wiles affect us less the next time he attacks. I remind you again that we do not war against flesh and blood. Our war is not against people, or against our circumstances, but against Satan, the true source of all misery.

Read Ephesians 5:15–20. List the things Paul says to do and not do.

_____

_____

_____

Take Action

List several ways you can keep from becoming lazy or passive about being watchful.

_____

_____

_____

How often do you hear biblical teaching about the wiles of the devil?

_____

What lessons can the foolish virgins and wise virgins teach you about staying watchful?

_____

_____

_____

Lazy people often run to active people and want them to give them what they worked hard for, but that is not God's way. We all have equal opportunity. God gives us what we need to work with, but if we won't do the work, then we miss out.

The parable ends with these strong words of advice: "Therefore, be on the alert [be prepared and ready], for you do not know the day nor the hour [when the Son of Man will come]" (Matt. 25:13).

In which areas do you need to be more watchful? How will you follow through with your goals? Write about this in each of the categories below. Your Thoughts:

_____

_____

_____

Temptations:

_____

_____

_____

Self or Selfishness:

_____

_____

_____

Remember

Remembering that we overcome evil with good is very important.

Be persistent and devoted to prayer, being alert and focused in your prayer life with an attitude of thanksgiving. (Colossians 4:2)

CHAPTER 13

"Self"

Before you begin, read Chapter 13 in Your Battles Belong to the Lord.

Get Started

How have you been watchful and alert to the devil's schemes this week?

_____

_____

_____

Read the opening Scripture, Philippians 2:4. How often do you think about other people and what they need?

_____

_____

_____

How selfish do you think you are? Explain.

_____

_____

_____

The devil tempts and provokes us to want to sin, but self makes the final choice and is therefore responsible when we do sin. When people are being selfish, they oppose God's will by exercising their own will and doing as they please. What they want is more important to them than what God wants.

Get Armed

How did selfishness cause the fall of Satan and Adam and Eve? (See Isa. 14:12–14 and Gen. 3:1–7.)

_____

_____

_____

_____

God created Satan perfectly, with unusual beauty and faculties. He had amazing abilities and great power. But he fell because of pride, which is nothing more than a manifestation of self. He wasn't satisfied with the amazing gifts and abilities God had bestowed on him; he wanted to be equal to—or above—God. He said that he would lift his throne above the throne of God (Isa. 14:13–14). Evil exists in this self, which is found in angelic beings as well as in people.

Think about free will. How is it a wonderful freedom and a great responsibility?

_____

_____

_____

_____

How often are you tempted to boast about your abilities? Why?

_____

_____

_____

_____

How can remembering that your ability comes from God help you avoid boasting or thinking of yourself more highly than others?

_____

_____

_____

The Word

Read Luke 22:24–30 and write about what's happening in your own words.

_____

_____

_____

_____

How were the disciples being selfish?

_____

_____

_____

_____

We may be surprised and disappointed by the disciples' behavior while not recognizing the selfishness in ourselves. Selfishness (self) is an inbred weakness in our flesh due to the fall of man. It will never completely disappear as long as we are on this earth, but we do not have to let it rule us. God has given us many tools with which to fight the enemy of self.

Read 2 Timothy 1:7. How can the spirit of discipline help us avoid selfishness?

_____

_____

_____

Read Galatians 5:22–23. How can the fruit of the Spirit help us overcome selfishness?

_____

_____

_____

What are some practical ways you can resist being selfish in your daily life?

_____

_____

_____

Read Galatians 2:20 from several translations. What is Paul saying in this verse?

_____

_____

_____

_____

Take Action

Do you believe that all disobedience is directly linked to selfishness? Explain why or why not.

_____

_____

_____

_____

How can you confront selfishness in your thoughts, desires, attitudes, and actions?

_____

_____

_____

_____

What are some ways you can be mindful to guard yourself against being selfish as you go through your day? Pray for God to help you establish a plan of action in this area.

_____

_____

_____

_____

Read the Scriptures listed in the book about Cain and Abel, Joseph and his brothers, and King David. Write what happened to them and how you can learn from their examples to help you avoid selfishness.

We cannot find a sin that was or is not committed because of self. We all have to deal with it, but we do not have to let it win the battle. If we are willing to die to self, as God's Word instructs us, we can be free from its tyranny.

Remember

Although Satan works hard to use the weakness of self against us, he cannot win if we are determined to follow God rather than self.

> Those who live according to the flesh have their minds set on what the flesh desires; but those who live in accordance with the Spirit have their minds set on what the Spirit desires. The mind governed by the flesh is death, but the mind governed by the Spirit is life and peace. (Romans 8:5–6 NIV)

Stand Still and See the Salvation of the Lord

Before you begin, read Chapter 14 in Your Battles Belong to the Lord.

Get Started

Write about how you've been more aware of selfishness and what you have done to overcome it since reading the previous chapter. Share what you want to continue to do.

_____

_____

_____

Read the opening quote by the unknown author. Do you agree or disagree? Why or why not?

_____

_____

_____

Moses gave the Israelites an instruction that would be life-changing for them if they would follow it—to "Stand still, and see the salvation of the Lord."

Get Armed

To better understand what Moses told the Israelites, read Exodus 14:1–14. Describe the situation they were in at that time.

_____

_____

_____

Fill in the blanks for Exodus 14:13–14, using the New King James Version.

And Moses said to the _____, "Do not be _____
_____. Stand _____, and see the _____
of the Lord, which He will accomplish for _____
today. For the Egyptians whom you see today, you shall see again
_____ more forever. The _____ will _____
for you, and you shall _____ your _____.

These verses remind us that our battles belong to the Lord and show us how to let Him fight them for us. First, we cannot run away from problems; we have to stand and face them. And second, we also have to move toward them in faith, trusting God to help us overcome them. "Don't run away, go forward" is a perfect picture of courage.

Write about a time you ran from a difficult or scary situation. What happened?

_____

_____

_____

The Word

Read about several other people in the Bible who ran from their problems. What happened?
Hagar (Genesis 16:1–13):

_____

_____

_____

Moses (Exodus 2:11–15; 3):

_____

_____

_____

Elijah (1 Kings 19:1–16):

_____

_____

_____

Jonah (Jonah 1–3):

_____

_____

_____

People run from difficulties for all kinds of reasons and in various ways. We may run from responsibility, accountability, hard work, difficult people, challenging places, our sin, ourselves, the truth, the past, and many other things. We may remove ourselves physically from a situation. We may stay too busy to deal with the problem, or we may try to escape it through substance abuse and addictions. But there are two ways we run that I want to discuss in greater detail—making excuses and blaming others.

Do you agree with the quote: "An excuse is nothing more than a reason stuffed with a lie"? Explain.

_____

_____

_____

What excuses have you made for not putting God first in your life or continuing to live with an unhealthy or ungodly behavior?

_____

_____

_____

_____

Write a prayer asking for forgiveness for making excuses.

_____

_____

_____

Take Action

Think about ways you will move forward and begin putting God first in your life. Write out a plan below.

_____

_____

_____

_____

Evaluate your actions this week. How often do you make excuses for not doing what you know in your heart you should do? How can you change your behavior?

_____

_____

_____

_____

The only way to prevent the devil from deceiving us is to always be willing to take responsibility for our actions no matter what others are doing. If you are looking for the perfect job or spouse, you are already deceived because the only perfect thing that exists is Jesus, and He wants to help us face and deal with the imperfect aspects of our lives in a loving, peaceful way.

Do you blame other people for your problems? Explain.

_____

_____

_____

_____

What can you do to stop blaming others?

_____

_____

_____

Use the lines below to reflect on anything you may be running from. Ask God to help you confront your issues.

_____

_____

_____

Remember

Deliverance comes when we learn to stand still (stop running) and confront the problems we prefer to avoid.

For with God nothing will be impossible. (Luke 1:37 NKJV)

CHAPTER 15
Spiritual Warfare God's Way, Part 1

Before you begin, read Chapter 15 in Your Battles Belong to the Lord.

Get Started

Have you faced anything that you were running from or blaming on someone or something else since reading the last chapter? Write about your situation below.

_____

_____

_____

Read the opening verse, Zechariah 4:6, from several translations. Rewrite the verse in your own words.

_____

_____

_____

Understanding or helping others understand how to fight against an invisible enemy with invisible weapons while wearing invisible armor is very challenging. The enemy, the weapons, and the armor are all undeniably real in the spiritual realm, but that realm cannot be seen with the natural eye unless, of course, God miraculously opens a person's eyes and allows a glimpse into it.

Get Armed

What type of "fruit" is evidence of the devil's activity in our world?

_____

_____

_____

What do you think Jesus meant in John 10:10 when He said, "The thief comes only in order to steal and kill and destroy"?

_____

_____

_____

What kind of life does Jesus say He came to give us? (See John 10:10.)

_____

_____

_____

What does that life look like to you?

_____

_____

_____

Are you enjoying that type of life now? Why or why not?

_____

_____

_____

Jesus didn't come simply to give us the promise of heaven when we die, but to give us a life worth living while we are on our way to heaven. Eternal life doesn't begin when we die; it starts the moment we are born again. Jesus came to give us victory and make us more than conquerors (see Rom. 8:37). He also came to destroy the works of the evil one (see 1 John 3:8), which does not mean to make them disappear, but to give us the strength to overcome them through our faith in Him.

Reflect on each strategy to defeat the devil discussed in this chapter and answer the following questions.

Worship

How can worship help you fight the spiritual war?

_____

_____

_____

Write down the names of several of your favorite worship songs. Add them to your playlist so they are readily available when you need to worship to fight spiritual warfare.

_____

_____

_____

What ways can you worship other than in song?

_____

_____

_____

Rest

What do you think it means to rest while being active?

_____

_____

_____

How well do you rest in God? Explain.

_____

_____

_____

Remain Calm in Adversity

Have you learned not to let difficulties disturb you? Explain why or why not.

_____

_____

_____

How can you remain calm in adversity?

_____

_____

_____

Stay Protected by God's Presence

Do you spend more time seeking God's presents or seeking God's presence?
Explain.

_____

_____

_____

Do you believe you need God more than you need what He can do for you?
Explain.

_____

_____

   Anything besides God that we feel we have to have to be satisfied is something the devil can use against us. We all want many things, but only one
thing is needful, and that is God Himself.

The Word

Read Acts 16:16–30 and answer the questions below.

Where were Paul and Silas going when they met the female slave?

_____

How was the slave profitable to others?

_____

Why was Paul annoyed by her?

_____

What did Paul do to stop her?

_____

Why did this displease her owners?

_____

_____

_____

How were Paul and Silas punished?

_____

_____

_____

How did Paul and Silas react after they were beaten and thrown in jail?

_____

_____

_____

Why did the jailer want to kill himself?

_____

_____

_____

Why did the jailer say he wanted to be saved?

_____

_____

_____

What lessons do Paul and Silas teach you about worship?

_____

_____

_____

Read Hebrews 4:10 from several translations. What does the verse mean to you?

_____

_____

_____

Read 2 Corinthians 4:8–10 and 16–18 from several translations of the Bible. In your own words, describe Paul's attitude about trials.

_____

_____

_____

Paul did not state that his trials were easy, but he did say that they did not make him worry, fear, become anxious, or despair. He endured difficulties, but he remained in God's rest. Going through a trial is enough to deal with on its own without having to worry and be anxious about it. Thank God for His gracious invitation to enter His rest!

Rest is warfare in the spiritual realm simply because Satan cannot understand how we can have such intense problems and rest in the midst of them. Jehoshaphat was delivered while worshipping and singing, and entering the rest of God does the same for us. We rest, God works, and we enjoy the benefit.

Do you believe God's presence is always with you? Why or why not? What Bible verses can you use to remember God's faithfulness to always be with you?

_____

_____

Take Action

Read the suggestions I make for how you can practice keeping God's presence a priority in your life. Write notes next to the ones you intend to incorporate into your life.

Practice seeking God for Who He is, not just for what He can do for you. You might even take a few days to avoid asking God for anything other than Himself.

_____

_____

_____

Start each day spending time with God in His Word or simply talking with Him. Tell Him you have no desire to do anything without Him and ask Him to make His presence real to you.

_____

_____

_____

_____

Stop what you're doing several times a day and remind yourself that God is with you right now! Tell God you need Him and appreciate His presence in your life.

_____

_____

_____

_____

Thank God throughout the day. There are hundreds of things we can thank Him for daily if we make a habit of doing so.

_____

_____

_____

_____

Write your own ideas about ways you can keep God's presence as a priority in your life.

_____

_____

_____

_____

Remember

Spending time with God, whether it is hours or even a few minutes, is a type of spiritual warfare, and it is very enjoyable.

He who dwells in the secret place of the Most High shall abide under the shadow of the Almighty. (Psalm 91:1 NKJV)

Spiritual Warfare God's Way, Part 2

Before you begin, read Chapter 16 in Your Battles Belong to the Lord.

Get Started

What strategies from the previous chapters have you intentionally practiced? Share what happened.

_____

_____

_____

_____

Which ones do you want to incorporate more into your life?

_____

_____

_____

Read James 4:7, the opening Scripture. Do you believe this verse? Why or why not?

_____

_____

_____

How can you submit yourself to God?

_____

_____

_____

Get Armed

Obedience

Think about the strategy of obedience. Evaluate your life and how obedient you are to God. Where do you need improvement?

_____

_____

_____

Actually, anytime we submit to God and do what He asks instead of doing what we may want to do, we engage in spiritual warfare. Satan hates it when we obey God, and our obedience is a powerful force against him.

One is to simply be obedient to God! All disobedience opens a door for the enemy and gives him access to our lives. This is especially the case if we are aware that what we are doing is against God's will and do it anyway.

How does Jesus serve as a model for us to be obedient to God?

_____

_____

_____

_____

Use the Power of Words

Do you believe words have power? Why or why not?

_____

_____

_____

Are there times when you intentionally remain quiet to fight battles? Explain.

_____

_____

_____

Love

What verses in the Bible about love stand out to you as good strategies to fight Satan?

_____

_____

_____

Love is not merely a word or a topic for a Sunday morning sermon; it is a power that can be seen and felt. Love takes action, and it has to flow in order to stay alive. We are never happier than when we are showing love to others. Most of us make the mistake of thinking happiness comes by getting everything we want, but that makes us selfish and miserable. Although it sounds like it couldn't work, the truth is that doing things for and giving to others is the source of true joy.

Overcome Evil with Good

How can doing good overcome evil?

_____

_____

_____

Why does it take intentionality, or a decision to do good on purpose, to love others when we are hurting? How do you do it?

_____

_____

_____

When Satan attacks, he expects to make us miserable and self-centered, but if we answer his attack with acts of kindness and meeting the needs of others, he becomes confused and then defeated. If we tend to God's business, which is loving people, then He will take care of ours. He will fight our battles and make sure we win.

The Word

Read 2 Corinthians 10:5. What does it say we are to do with our thoughts? How are we to do this?

_____

_____

_____

Read John 14:15. Why do you think love and obedience go hand in hand?

_____

_____

_____

Read Jeremiah 23:28 from several translations of the Bible. What does the verse say about how we should speak?

_____

_____

_____

Read Hebrews 4:12. How is the Word of God like a sword?

_____

_____

_____

Read Ephesians 4:26–27. How do you think we can feel anger yet not sin?

_____

_____

_____

Take Action

Do you find it hard to forgive? Explain why or why not.

_____

_____

_____

What strategies can you incorporate into your life to remind you to let go of anger and unforgiveness?

_____

_____

_____

Review the other strategies discussed in this chapter. Which ones will you be intentional about working on and how?

_____

_____

_____

Remember

Start fighting with love and forgiveness, and you will easily defeat the devil.

If you forgive someone, I also forgive him. And what I have forgiven— if I had anything to forgive—I forgave it for you, as if Christ were with me. I did this so that Satan would not win anything from us, because we know very well what Satan's plans are. (2 Corinthians 2:10–11 NCV)

The Power of a Thankful Life

Before you begin, read Chapter 17 of Your Battles Belong to the Lord.

Get Started

Think about the strategies from the previous two chapters. Which ones have been helpful in defeating the devil? Which ones would you like to incorporate more into your life?

_____

_____

_____

Read 2 Chronicles 20 to review the story of Jehoshaphat. What did those appointed to sing praises to the Lord say?

_____

_____

_____

What does it mean to you that God's steadfast love endures forever?

_____

_____

_____

Get Armed

The power of praise and worship is amazing, as is the giving of thanks. We are to "be thankful and say so" (Psalm 100:4 AMPC). Apparently voicing thankfulness is important. Try taking one whole day each week and thank God for things like clean water, a warm home in the winter, food to eat, friends and family to love, and thousands of other things we can easily take for granted unless we purpose to recognize and be thankful for them.

List ten things you are thankful for today. Keep adding to the list throughout your day or week.

_____

_____

_____

How often do you count your blessings? How can counting your blessings keep you from taking them for granted?

_____

_____

_____

_____

Think about how much you give thanks versus how much you complain. Which one do you do more? Why?

_____

_____

_____

Do you find your joy increasing when you focus on things you have to be thankful for rather than the inconveniences and challenges you encounter? Why or why not?

_____

_____

_____

I doubt that any of us can even imagine how powerful our lives would be if we lived daily with hearts filled with gratitude. But even if we have made mistakes in the past by complaining too much and not being thankful enough, we can have a new beginning and it can start today.

The Word

Read 1 Corinthians 10:8–10. Write down what happened to the people who complained.

_____

In your own words, describe what the following verses say about complaining.

James 5:9:

_____

_____

_____

1 Peter 4:8–9:

_____

_____

_____

What did God instruct Habakkuk and Nehemiah to do when they came to Him with complaints? What can you learn from their example?

Habakkuk 2:2:

_____

_____

_____

Nehemiah 2:4–18:

_____

_____

_____

We cannot complain ourselves into a better position in life. We should pray, be thankful for what we do have, and ask God to show us what He wants us to do to make our situation better.

Read Philippians 2:14–15 from several translations. Rewrite these verses in your own words.

_____

_____

_____

Take Action

Think of ways being thankful has impacted your life. Write about your experiences for each statement below.

Thanksgiving protects you.

_____

_____

_____

Thanksgiving strengthens you.

_____

_____

_____

Thanksgiving increases your faith.

_____

_____

_____

Thanksgiving is the expression of joy God-ward, and is therefore a fruit of the Spirit (see Gal. 5:22–23). Believers are encouraged to abound in it (see Col. 2:7). We are not to be a little thankful, but to abound and overflow with thankfulness.

How do we give God a "sacrifice of praise"?

_____

_____

_____

A sacrifice often denotes giving up something. Give up complaining and instead find something to be thankful for in every situation.

Remember

God offers us an opportunity to shine brightly for Him by simply refusing to complain.

Give thanks in all circumstances; for this is the will of God in Christ Jesus for you. Do not quench the Spirit. (1 Thessalonians 5:18–19 ESV)

A Beautiful Mind

Before you begin, read Chapter 18 in Your Battles Belong to the Lord.

Get Started

Since completing the previous chapter, are you giving more thanks to God and complaining less? Share what has happened.

_____

_____

_____

_____

_____

Read the opening Scripture, 2 Corinthians 11:3. What is Paul, the writer, afraid will happen to the people?

_____

_____

_____

_____

Christianity is simple, but the devil works to turn it into something complex, difficult, and confusing. We are to be on our guard against our powerful adversary, and anytime we find ourselves confused, we should remember that God is not a God of confusion (see 1 Cor. 14:33). We are to beware so no one will deceive us or take us captive by philosophy (see Col. 2:8).

Get Armed

Why can being addicted to reasoning be dangerous for Christians?

_____

_____

_____

Do you agree that Christianity is simple? Explain why or why not.

_____

_____

_____

Why is it dangerous to lean too heavily on our own knowledge?

_____

_____

_____

How does pride cause us to be deceived by the enemy?

_____

_____

_____

God wants us to seek knowledge of Him and His principles. Because humanity is fallen, this great gift of the mind and its ability to retain knowledge often makes people proud, even to the point that they think they know more than they do. The devil has always attacked people in their thinking. He also attacks our emotions and our will, but our minds are his favorite target. We should seek to keep our minds filled with beautiful, good, peaceful thoughts.

Explain what this statement means: "The wisest person in the world is the one who understands that he will never understand everything."

_____

_____

_____

How can you apply that quote to your life?

_____

_____

_____

The Word

Read 1 Corinthians 14:33 in several translations. What does it mean that God is not the author of confusion?

_____

_____

_____

Read 1 Corinthians 13:9–10. What does verse 10 explain to us about our ability to understand everything about God and this life?

_____

_____

_____

According to Deuteronomy 29:29, what does God choose to reveal to us? Why is our faith in Him critical when it comes to being satisfied with what we can understand?

_____

_____

_____

Read 1 Timothy 3:16. What is "the mystery [the hidden truth] of godliness"?

_____

_____

_____

If you knew everything about God, how would that affect your relationship with Him?

_____

_____

_____

How does this fit into letting God fight our battles? It partially depends on whether or not we can believe what the Word of God says even when life seems to make no sense. If we cannot do that, then we end up fighting battle after battle in our own minds and becoming more and more confused. To have a painful problem is miserable, but to be confused about the problem adds another layer of pain. Psalm 37:3 offers God's answer to problems that seem unfair: "Trust in the Lord, and do good" (ESV). This verse promises that even though the wicked seem to prosper for a time, their end will come and the righteous will inherit the earth. Faith invites us to look beyond what is happening right now to the glorious future God has promised us.

Take Action

How can you deal with not knowing everything, especially when it comes to tragedies?

_____

_____

_____

How has Satan tried to use reasoning to get you off track?

_____

_____

_____

Our lives would be so much sweeter and easier if we would simply believe what God says whether it makes sense to our minds or not. Some of us have no problem doing that, but highly intelligent people might. I am not saying they will definitely have problems, but it is a possible danger to watch out for.

Write Proverbs 3:5–7 in your own words.

_____

_____

_____

Consider posting Proverbs 3:5–7 in your own words in an area where you'll see it often. It is also a good passage of Scripture to commit to memory.

Pride was Satan's downfall (see Isa. 14:13–14), and it will be ours also if we allow it into our thinking. Pride causes us to lift ourselves up and put others down, and it causes us to devalue people Jesus deems valuable enough to die for.

Remember

Christ is our wisdom from God, and as long as we follow Him, we will be wise men and women.

Trust in the Lord with all your heart and lean not on your own understanding; in all your ways submit to him, and he will make your paths straight. (Proverbs 3:5–6 NIV)

Breaking Satan's Assignment

Before you begin, read Chapter 19 in Your Battles Belong to the Lord.

Get Started

Have you changed anything since studying the previous chapter on reasoning and the problem of trying to know everything? Explain what has happened.

_____

_____

_____

Read the opening Scripture, Proverbs 25:28, from several versions of the Bible. What does it say about a person who doesn't have self-control? What do you think the analogy means?

_____

_____

_____

Consider drawing an illustration to show what a person without self-control looks like.

Satan is carrying out an assignment against us, but we need not be concerned because we have the power through Christ to break that assignment. Jesus said that the thief (Satan) comes for one purpose—to steal, kill, and destroy (see John 10:10). Whether he wants to steal our dreams for our lives, our confidence, our relationship with God, our friendships, our joy, or our peace, he is a thief!

Get Armed

What are some things you have witnessed Satan trying to steal, kill, or destroy? Explain.

_____

_____

_____

Do you believe that the One in you is greater than the devil? Explain why or why not.

_____

_____

_____

How can self-control and discipline serve as an effective strategy against the devil?

_____

_____

_____

1 Peter 5:8 teaches us to be well balanced because our adversary, the devil, roams around like a hungry lion seeking someone to devour.

Living a balanced life is impossible without self-control and the ability to discipline our thoughts, emotions, and choices. It also requires regular examination of our lives and asking God to reveal any area that may be out of balance. If He does, it requires us to take action to correct any excess.

In your own words, describe what a balanced life looks like.

_____

_____

_____

Consider drawing an illustration to show balance.

What could you be doing too much of in your life? Too little?

_____

_____

_____

_____

How can you achieve a right balance in every area of your life? Be specific and list practical ways you can go about this.

_____

_____

_____

_____

The Word

Read Galatians 5:22–23 from several translations. List the fruit of the Spirit and include your own description of each characteristic in your own words.

_____

_____

_____

Which fruit of the Spirit do you need more in your life? How can you begin developing more of these character traits that reflect the nature of Christ?

_____

_____

_____

_____

We are complex beings with minds that think, emotions that feel, and wills that want. We also have bodies that get tired, lazy, and hungry. They don't always cooperate willingly with what we want to do, so we have to use the discipline and self-control God has given us. People who always do what they feel like doing play right into the devil's hand, and if they continue, their lives will amount to nothing. Our feelings are a driving factor in our lives, and we are often tempted to let them rule us, but we must not. Satan uses our feelings against us by causing us to think we must feel like doing something in order to do it, but that is incorrect. We learn to live by principle rather than by our feelings. We should set godly standards for our lives and discipline ourselves to follow them. We cannot follow every thought we think because many of our thoughts are dropped into our minds by the devil and would lead us down paths of destruction, so we must also discipline our thoughts and control them.

Read Philippians 4:8 NIV and fill in the blanks.

Finally, brothers and sisters, whatever is _____, what is _____, whatever is _____, whatever is _____, whatever is _____, whatever is _____—if anything is _____ or _____—think about such things.

Focus on 1 Corinthians 9:27 and 10:23, and ask yourself what true freedom really looks like and how we attain it.

Take Action

How often do you try to control all of your circumstances, and how does it actually impact yourself and others?

_____

_____

How can focusing on controlling yourself rather than circumstances help?

_____

_____

Do you agree that the main reason we try to control others and circumstances is because we are selfish and afraid we won't get what we want? Explain.

_____

_____

Do you try to control things or others because you have been hurt in the past or treated unjustly? If so, how can you change this?

_____

_____

How can you practice exercising self-control? Circle the areas that impact you the most and write practical steps you can take to manage them the way God is leading you to do so.

Words

_____

_____

Finances

_____

_____

Time

_____

_____

Appetite

_____

_____

_____

Our bodies are temples of the Holy Spirit (see 1 Cor. 6:19), and as such, we should discipline ourselves to be healthy houses for Him to dwell in. Not everyone will be skinny, just as not everyone will be tall, but we should maintain balance concerning food, and eat and enjoy what we need without overeating. This is not meant to condemn people who weigh more than they should, but it is an encouragement to value yourself enough to be as healthy as you can be.

Explain what this statement means: "The discomfort of discipline pales in comparison to the ultimate discomfort of being undisciplined."

_____

_____

_____

How can remembering the above help you in your motivation to exercise self-control?

_____

_____

_____

Remember

I believe God has given us self-control as a gift to help us live balanced lives, and I urge you to value the gift.

But the fruit of the Spirit is love, joy, peace, forbearance, kindness, goodness, faithfulness, gentleness and self-control. Against such things there is no law. (Galatians 5:22–23 NIV)

Internal Rest

Before you begin, read Chapter 20 in Your Battles Belong to the Lord.

Get Started

Review your notes on self-control from the previous chapter. Evaluate yourself on a scale of 1 to 5 (with 5 being the most self-controlled) to determine the progress you've made in this area. How much have you exercised self-control since reading the chapter? What can you do to get closer to 5 or to remain at 5?

```
  ┌────┬────┬────┬────┐
  1    2    3    4    5
```

_____

_____

_____

Meditate on the opening Scripture, Matthew 11:29. What does it mean to take Jesus' yoke upon you? What does Jesus promise you will find when you do?

_____

_____

_____

It is fairly easy to adjust our schedules to enable ourselves to get more physical rest, but we can lie on a beach in the sun all day and still not rest because we are not resting our souls. We can be in bed and still worry, try to figure out solutions to problems or endeavor to fix situations that are not even our responsibilities.

Get Armed

What do you think it means to rest internally?

_____

_____

_____

What are practical ways you can rest internally?

_____

_____

_____

Do you think you need to rest more internally? Explain?

_____

_____

_____

_____

What do you think I mean by this statement: "The kind of rest Jesus offers us is not rest *from* work but rest *in* work."

_____

_____

_____

How can Jesus offer us this type of rest?

_____

_____

_____

_____

The more we can develop and maintain the type of rest Jesus offers us, the easier life becomes and the more we release God to fight our battles for us instead of always feeling like we are personally fighting something.

The Word

Read 1 Peter 5:7 from several translations. Write what the verse says to you in your own words.

_____

_____

_____

_____

How often do you truly cast your cares, worries, or anxieties upon God?

_____

_____

_____

Memorize a version of 1 Peter 5:7 and repeat it several times throughout the day to remind yourself to give God all of your worries and concerns.
Study Matthew 6:25–34. What is this passage saying to you about worry?

_____

_____

_____

_____

How do we show humility by casting all cares upon God?

_____

_____

_____

_____

Think of a situation in your life that is frustrating you. Ask yourself: Is there anything I can do about that situation? If so, what will you do?

_____

_____

_____

If the answer is no, how will you cast your frustration upon God?

_____

_____

_____

By nature I would tend to be a worrier because I am a "fixer." I want to fix problems. Nothing is more frustrating to me than a problem I cannot fix, so I have had to learn to take the same advice I am offering to you.

Take Action

Do you feel responsible for other people? If so, do you have a false sense of responsibility for anyone in any of those relationships? Explain.

_____

_____

_____

Read what I share about my worrying about the people in the nail salon. How did this cause me to be stressed and ruin my internal rest, especially during a treatment that was supposed to be relaxing?

_____

_____

_____

Have you ever found yourself in a similar situation? Explain.

_____

_____

_____

How can you take responsibility only for things you are responsible for?

_____

_____

_____

One thing we must do in order not to worry is to learn to deal with our lives as they are and not as we would like them to be. The same approach goes for the people in our lives. We must learn to love them as they are, and not the way we would like them to be. Some of the writers from the sixteenth and seventeenth centuries wrote about "acceptance with joy," meaning that if a situation wasn't going to change, they learned to accept it and remain joyful. Doing so doesn't mean nothing will ever change, but it does mean that for the present time we trust God's will and timing in every situation. We simply cannot base our joy and peace on our circumstances. If we do, the devil can manipulate them continually, causing us to be upset most of the time. Whatever we might be going through at any given time will pass, and until it does, we can decide to enjoy our lives and keep our peace.

How can you handle mistakes from the past that may pop up in your mind and threaten internal rest?

_____

_____

_____

How can you prevent thoughts of the future from robbing you of internal rest?

_____

_____

_____

I have lost a great deal of my life spending the present day living in the past or in the future. I don't do that now, but I did for many years, and I pray you will not do as I did. Although there are many things I wish I had done differently, I cannot go back and redo them, so I refuse to lose another day being anxious and worried about them. God can fight the battles of our past mistakes and actually work them for our good if we will release them to Him. How can you look forward to your future with anticipation and joy rather than fear and anxiety?

_____

_____

_____

_____

Remember

God wants to and will fight our battles for us. Without Him, we won't win them anyway, but we have to release them to Him if we want the victory only He can give.

Give all your worries and cares to God, for he cares about you. (1 Peter 5:7 NLT)

Protecting Yourself from Satan, the Thief

Before you begin, read Chapter 21 in Your Battles Belong to the Lord.

Get Started

Have you enjoyed more internal rest as a result of what you learned in the previous chapter? Explain why or why not.

_____

_____

_____

What more would you like to do, or not do, to gain internal rest?

_____

_____

_____

Read John 10:10. What does Jesus promise to give us?

_____

_____

_____

Do you believe you are enjoying abundant life right now? Explain why or why not.

_____

_____

_____

We are supposed to do good works, but we don't do them to gain acceptance or love from God. We do them because in His grace and mercy He has provided acceptance to us as an unconditional gift. Our obedience should be a response to God's goodness, not an effort to gain anything from Him.

Satan delights in deceiving people in this area. By doing so, he can turn people into legalists—people who work hard to follow every rule, make sure they read certain amounts of Scripture daily, pray for specified lengths of time, and do good works, but sadly, do it all with the wrong motive.

Get Armed

We've studied a lot about Satan and his desire to steal from us. What have you realized Satan is trying to steal from you personally?

_____

_____

_____

How will you defeat Satan?

_____

_____

_____

What is real Christianity? How are we forgiven of our sins and born again?

_____

_____

_____

Do you have true faith in Jesus? Explain.

_____

_____

If you are not sure about your relationship with Christ, please write your concerns below and talk with your pastor or someone you trust who believes God's Word as soon as possible.

_____

_____

_____

What does this statement mean: "Our obedience should be a response to God's goodness, not an effort to gain anything from Him."

_____

_____

_____

Why do you do good works?

_____

_____

_____

Do you struggle with legalism? Or have you struggled in the past? Why or why not?

_____

_____

_____

I remember the agony of my struggles in the early years of my walk with God. I truly loved the Lord, but Satan had deceived me through the lies he told me about my duty as a Christian. I thought, as millions of others do, that regular church attendance, reading the Bible a little each day and saying some prayers, along with confessing my sins, summed up what I needed to do. I also believed I needed to do some good works, so I joined the evangelism team of our church. But God had not given me the grace for door-to-door evangelism, so I dreaded it every week.

The Word

What does Galatians 3:10 say about depending on the Law and what does it mean?

_____

_____

_____

_____

What does Philippians 1:6 say and how can it help prevent legalism?

_____

_____

_____

Read Romans 8:1–2. What is condemnation? How are we set free from it?

_____

_____

_____

What does Romans 8:1–2 mean to you?

_____

_____

_____

The Old Covenant required people to follow rules and regulations and to make sacrifices for their sins, but Jesus offers us a New Covenant under which the law is written in our hearts (see Heb. 8:10). We can now follow the Holy Spirit and be assured of doing the right thing. He has given us His Spirit and has put His heart in us. He is the one and only sacrifice that was ever needed for all time. When we fail, we no longer need to try to do good things to make up for our mistakes. All we need to do is look to the cross of Calvary, where Jesus paid for our sins once and for all (see Heb. 9:12). Under the New Covenant, when we confess our sins and turn from them, He forgives them, forgets them, and remembers them no more (see Heb. 8:12; 10:16–18).

What is the difference between your "want to" and believing you "have to" do something?

_____

_____

_____

How has Jesus changed "have to" to "want to" in your life?

_____

_____

Take Action

Listen to what you say this week. Recall how many times you say you "have" to do something. Write down what you said. How might you change those "have-to's" to something more truthful?

_____

_____

_____

Those who live under the law are always frustrated simply because God will not allow us to get what we want from Him through our own struggle and effort. He requires that we come to Him in faith.

How can simply changing your language help you enjoy life more?

_____

_____

_____

Study Matthew 23 in several translations. Write down some of the things Jesus accused the Pharisees of. How might you do some of those same things? After studying this passage, what needs to change in your heart?

_____

_____

_____

_____

God looks at our hearts more than He looks at our performances. Write a prayer, asking God to work in your heart in the areas where you want to become more like Christ. Be honest about your weaknesses and faults. Remember, God loves you unconditionally and He wants to help you!

_____

_____

_____

_____

Being a Christian should be a powerful experience. Paul also prayed that he would know Christ and the power of His resurrection, which lifted Him out from among the dead while still in the body (see Phil. 3:10). This is the kind of power we should also experience.

As believers in Christ, we should have the power to endure hardship without losing our joy or complaining.

Do you think you can endure hardships without losing your joy? Explain.

Are you enjoying a close, personal, intimate relationship with God? How do you relate to Him?

Remember

Try focusing on your relationship with the Lord more than on keeping rules and laws, and you will find that the desire to do the right thing will begin to fill your heart and you will do what is right with ease.

"The thief comes only to steal and kill and destroy; I have come that they may have life, and have it to the full." (John 10:10 NIV)

God Always Gives Us the Victory

Before you begin, read Chapter 22 in Your Battles Belong to the Lord.

Get Started

Since reading the previous chapter—and the entire book—how have you focused more on your relationship with God rather than on religious rules? Do you think you are living the abundant life Jesus came to give you? Why or why not?

_____

_____

_____

_____

Read the opening Scripture, Psalm 34:19. What does this verse say to you about life in Christ?

_____

_____

_____

Write a praise song or note of thanksgiving to God for promising to rescue you from all of your hardships.

_____

_____

_____

Although we do go through many difficulties in life, we can take comfort in God's promise to give us victory (see 1 Cor. 15:57). We can always have hope, which is the confident expectation that something good is going to happen in our lives.

Get Armed

Read 1 Corinthians 15:54–58. What does death mean for believers in Christ? How do we have victory over death?

_____

_____

_____

In verse 58, what does *standing firm* mean to you?

_____

_____

_____

What have you learned about the devil and his strategies of attack since studying this book?

_____

_____

_____

How will these insights help you overcome him moving forward?

_____

_____

_____

Satan provokes times of pain and misery in our lives and wants to use them to discourage us and draw us away from God. He will attempt to make us think God doesn't love us, especially if the suffering lasts a long time.

Satan will also attempt to make us think we have sinned in some way, so God must be punishing us through our suffering. Although there are times when hidden personal sin can open a door for Satan to wreak havoc in our lives, that is not always the case. We live in a world full of sin and its results, and Jesus tells us we will have tribulation in the world (see John 16:33). Nowhere does Scripture promise us a life free from suffering. We do, however, have the promise that God will be with us always, that He will rescue us, and that He will work good out of all things if we love Him and want His will (see Rom. 8:28).

The Word

What promises in the Word of God can help you through difficult times?

_____

_____

_____

How can these verses help you overcome difficulties?

_____

_____

_____

Consider writing these verses on cards and sharing them with someone in your life who is going through a tough time. Keep a set for yourself to review often.

Read Hebrews 4:14–16. How does it help you in times of trouble to remember that Jesus, our High Priest, knows exactly how we feel when we're hurting or suffering?

_____

_____

_____

Have you ever felt like you were not going to make it through a tragedy or stressful time? What happened?

_____

_____

_____

How can recalling how God brought you through that circumstance help you in times of trouble?

_____

_____

_____

What story from the Bible reminds you that God helps us in times of trouble?

_____

_____

_____

Make time to reread that story this week. Write down any new insights you find on how the person encourages you.

_____

_____

_____

_____

When Jesus ascended to the right hand of the Father, He sent us an Encourager, the Holy Spirit, to represent Him and work with us on His behalf (see Acts 2:33). The Holy Spirit is also called the Comforter (see John 15:26). He is with us to help us, to counsel and to comfort us. He will keep us from discouragement if we will listen to Him. He may encourage us directly in some way or He may—and often does—work through other people to encourage us. God has an antidote for every evil thing the enemy tries to do. All we need to do is discover what it is and apply it in our lives. The devil discourages, but the Holy Spirit encourages. The devil tries to destroy, but God restores, renews, and rebuilds. The devil is a liar, but God is Truth.

How does David's example in Psalm 42 help you know how to fight discouragement?

_____

_____

_____

Take Action

Always remember that the devil is persistent, and we will need to be equally persistent if we intend to overcome him.

In what ways will you be persistent in resisting the devil in your daily life?

_____

_____

_____

_____

How can knowing yourself help you guard against Satan's attacks? In what areas does the enemy try to attack you?

_____

_____

_____

_____

What strategies from this book will help you fight Satan?

_____

_____

_____

_____

Read "Why Would God Want Me?" What can you learn from the not-so-perfect people in the Bible?

_____

_____

_____

Don't let your deficits stop you from following God's lead. We all have deficits or reasons God should not choose us, yet He chooses us all the same. Reflect on these statements and write your thoughts below.

_____

_____

_____

What do these statements mean to you: "Satan looks back and sees our mistakes. God looks back and sees the Cross."

_____

_____

_____

Draw an illustration to remind you of this truth.

Do you believe trials make us stronger? Explain why or why not.

_____

_____

What trial in your life has made you stronger?

_____

_____

_____

I realize that the devil hates it when we show love or try to help people in need, or when the gospel is preached and people are being saved. He may hate it and try to stir up trouble, but the battle is already won. We learn endurance as we go through trials and tribulations. In simple terms, I think this means that we learn to outlast the devil. Just as he left Jesus in the wilderness after he had finished testing Him, saying he would wait for a more opportune time, so will he leave us if we stand firm on God's Word as Jesus did (see Luke 4:1–13). The devil will wait for another opportunity, but we need not fear because the battle belongs to the Lord and we are more than conquerors through Christ, who loves us (see Rom. 8:37).

Have you learned the truth of the title of this book—that your battles belong to God? Explain.

_____

_____

_____

_____

Thanks be to God, who always gives us the victory through Jesus Christ our Lord!

Think of a way you will give thanks to God for victory in your life. You may decide to write a prayer or song of thanksgiving, draw or create something for someone else, or perform an act of kindness as a way of showing thanks to God. Write your ideas below...and go out and share the love of Christ with others as God fights your battles!

_____

_____

_____

_____

Remember

Your battles belong to the Lord!

I have told you these things, so that in me you may have peace. In this world you will have trouble. But take heart! I have overcome the world. (John 16:33 NIV)

Do you have a real relationship with Jesus?

God loves you! He created you to be a special, unique, one-of-a-kind individual, and He has a specific purpose and plan for your life. And through a personal relationship with your Creator—God—you can discover a way of life that will truly satisfy your soul.

No matter who you are, what you've done, or where you are in your life right now, God's love and grace are greater than your sin—your mistakes. Jesus willingly gave His life so you can receive forgiveness from God and have new life in Him. He's just waiting for you to invite Him to be your Savior and Lord.

If you are ready to commit your life to Jesus and follow Him, all you have to do is ask Him to forgive your sins and give you a fresh start in the life you are meant to live. Begin by praying this prayer...

Lord Jesus, thank You for giving Your life for me and forgiving me of my sins so I can have a personal relationship with You. I am sincerely sorry for the mistakes I've made, and I know I need You to help me live right.

Your Word says in Romans 10:9, "If you declare with your mouth, 'Jesus is Lord,' and believe in your heart that God raised him from the dead, you will be saved" (NIV). I believe You are the Son of God and confess You as my Savior and Lord. Take me just as I am, and work in my heart, making me the person You want me to be. I want to live for You, Jesus, and I am so grateful that You are giving me a fresh start in my new life with You today.

I love You, Jesus!

It's so amazing to know that God loves us so much! He wants to have a deep, intimate relationship with us that grows every day as we spend time with Him in prayer and Bible study. And we want to encourage you in your new life in Christ.

Please visit joycemeyer.org/salvation to request Joyce's book *A New Way of Living*, which is our gift to you. We also have other free resources online to help you make progress in pursuing everything God has for you.

Congratulations on your fresh start in your life in Christ! We hope to hear from you soon.

ABOUT THE AUTHOR

JOYCE MEYER is one of the world's leading practical Bible teachers. A *New York Times* bestselling author, Joyce's books have helped millions of people find hope and restoration through Jesus Christ. Joyce's programs, *Enjoying Everyday Life* and *Everyday Answers with Joyce Meyer*, air around the world on television, radio, and the Internet. Through Joyce Meyer Ministries, Joyce teaches internationally on a number of topics with a particular focus on how the Word of God applies to our everyday lives. Her candid communication style allows her to share openly and practically about her experiences so others can apply what she has learned to their lives.

Joyce has authored more than 100 books, which have been translated into more than 100 languages, and over 65 million of her books have been distributed worldwide. Bestsellers include *Power Thoughts*; *The Confident Woman*; *Look Great, Feel Great*; *Starting Your Day Right*; *Ending Your Day Right*; *Approval Addiction*; *How to Hear from God*; *Beauty for Ashes*; and *Battlefield of the Mind*.

Joyce's passion to help hurting people is foundational to the vision of Hand of Hope, the missions arm of Joyce Meyer Ministries. Hand of Hope provides worldwide humanitarian outreaches such as feeding programs, medical care, orphanages, disaster response, human trafficking intervention and rehabilitation, and much more—always sharing the love and Gospel of Christ.

JOYCE MEYER MINISTRIES
U.S. & FOREIGN OFFICE ADDRESSES

Joyce Meyer Ministries
P.O. Box 655
Fenton, MO 63026
USA
(636) 349-0303

Joyce Meyer Ministries—Canada
P.O. Box 7700
Vancouver, BC V6B 4E2
Canada
(800) 868-1002

Joyce Meyer Ministries—Australia
Locked Bag 77
Mansfield Delivery Centre
Queensland 4122
Australia
(07) 3349 1200

Joyce Meyer Ministries—England
P.O. Box 1549
Windsor SL4 1GT
United Kingdom
01753 831102

Joyce Meyer Ministries—South Africa
P.O. Box 5
Cape Town 8000
South Africa
(27) 21-701-1056

OTHER BOOKS BY JOYCE MEYER

100 Ways to Simplify Your Life
21 Ways to Finding Peace and Happiness
Any Minute
Approval Addiction
The Approval Fix
The Battle Belongs to the Lord
Battlefield of the Mind*
Battlefield of the Mind for Kids
Battlefield of the Mind for Teens
Battlefield of the Mind Devotional
Be Anxious for Nothing*
Being the Person God Made You to Be
Beauty for Ashes
Change Your Words, Change Your Life
The Confident Mom
The Confident Woman
The Confident Woman Devotional
Do Yourself a Favor . . . Forgive
Eat the Cookie . . . Buy the Shoes
Eight Ways to Keep the Devil Under Your Feet
Ending Your Day Right
Enjoying Where You Are on the Way to Where You Are Going
Ephesians: Biblical Commentary
The Everyday Life Bible
Filled with the Spirit
Good Health, Good Life
Healing the Soul of a Woman*
Hearing from God Each Morning
How to Hear from God*
How to Succeed at Being Yourself
I Dare You
If Not for the Grace of God*
In Pursuit of Peace
James: Biblical Commentary
The Joy of Believing Prayer
Knowing God Intimately
A Leader in the Making
Life in the Word
Living Beyond Your Feelings
Living Courageously
Look Great, Feel Great

Love Out Loud
The Love Revolution
Making Good Habits, Breaking Bad Habits
Making Marriage Work (previously published as Help Me—I'm Married!)
Me and My Big Mouth!*
The Mind Connection*
Never Give Up!
Never Lose Heart
New Day, New You
Overload
The Penny
Perfect Love (previously published as God Is Not Mad at You)*
The Power of Being Positive
The Power of Being Thankful
The Power of Determination
The Power of Forgiveness
The Power of Simple Prayer
Power Thoughts
Power Thoughts Devotional
Reduce Me to Love
The Secret Power of Speaking God's Word
The Secrets of Spiritual Power
The Secret to True Happiness
Seven Things That Steal Your Joy
Start Your New Life Today
Starting Your Day Right
Straight Talk
Teenagers Are People Too!
Trusting God Day by Day
The Word, the Name, the Blood
Woman to Woman
You Can Begin Again

JOYCE MEYER SPANISH TITLES

Belleza en Lugar de Cenizas (Beauty for Ashes)
Buena Salud, Buena Vida (Good Health, Good Life)
Cambia Tus Palabras, Cambia Tu Vida (Change Your Words, Change Your Life)
El Campo de Batalla de la Mente (Battlefield of the Mind)
Como Formar Buenos Habitos y Romper Malos Habitos (Making Good Habits,
Breaking Bad Habits)
La Conexión de la Mente (The Mind Connection)

Dios No Está Enojado Contigo (God Is Not Mad at You)
La Dosis de Aprobación (The Approval Fix)
Efesios: Comentario Biblico (Ephesians: Biblical Commentary)
Empezando Tu Día Bien (Starting Your Day Right)
Hazte un Favor a Ti Mismo...Perdona (Do Yourself a Favor...Forgive)
Madre Segura de Sí Misma (The Confident Mom)
Pensamientos de Poder (Power Thoughts)
Sanidad para el Alma de una Mujer (Healing the Soul of a Woman)
Santiago: Comentario Bíblico (James: Biblical Commentary)
Sobrecarga (Overload)*
Termina Bien Tu Día (Ending Your Day Right)
Usted Puede Comenzar de Nuevo (You Can Begin Again)
Viva Valientemente (Living Courageously)

*Study Guide available for this title.

BOOKS BY DAVE MEYER

Life Lines

235
.4
MEY

Meyer, J.
Your battles belong to the Lord
study guide.
Aurora P.L. JAN20
33164300653198